THE  TIMES

getting a **TOP JOB** in
... **SALES & BUSINESS**
DEVELOPMENT

patrick forsyth

**KOGAN
PAGE**

Life is what happens while you are making other plans.

John Lennon

First published in 2002

Kogan Page Limited
120 Pentonville Road
London N1 9JN

British Library Cataloguing in Publication Data

A CIP record for this book is available from the British Library.

ISBN 0 7494 3724 3

Typeset by Saxon Graphics Ltd, Derby
Printed and bound in Great Britain by Clays Ltd, St Ives plc

Contents

The author

Patrick Forsyth has had a successful career in marketing, or certainly he likes to think so. He now runs his own company, Touchstone Training & Consultancy, specialising in the improvement of marketing, sales and communication and management skills, and says he has now 'found an employer I can really get on with'.

He began his career in publishing (well, books seemed an interesting product), and worked happily in sales, in promotion and marketing there before escaping to something better paid just ahead of terminal poverty. He then worked for the Institute of Marketing (now the Chartered Institute) first in research, latterly in the promotion of their training products and publications. He helped set up an export assistance scheme and then moved into consultancy, first in a line management marketing position. Much against his better judgement initially, he was soon persuaded to get involved in client work and began to undertake consulting assignments and conduct training courses.

His work also began to take on an international dimension. He helped set up offices in Brussels and Singapore and began to work and lecture overseas. He still travels regularly, especially to South East Asia, and has, over the years, worked in most countries in continental Europe, including the old Eastern bloc. Other, more occasional, visits have included the USA, Australia, East Africa, Argentina and Borneo.

After some years at Director level in a medium-sized marketing consultancy, he set up his own organisation in 1990. He conducts training for organisations in a wide range of industries, and has conducted public courses for such bodies as the Institute of Management, the City University Business School and the London Chamber of Commerce.

In addition, he writes on management and marketing issues in a variety of business journals and is the author of more than 30 business books (with titles published in more than a dozen languages). He has also written material to accompany a variety of training packages (audio, video, etc) and has appeared on television discussing marketing and management.

Foreword

Business people the world over recognise the key role of sales at the leading edge of the commercial process. But this role is more respected in some countries than others and the attitude in Britain is revealed by our own peculiar euphemisms: Business Development, Client Service Manager, even saying 'Marketing' when we mean 'Sales'.

Not so long ago the main attributes of a salesperson – who was almost certainly male – were to be presentable and articulate. Today sales people need a full portfolio of technical, managerial and communication skills as well as a clear understanding of how they fit into the team that makes up a modern organisation.

Sales teams grapple with many other issues: compliance, sustainability and ethics, for example and there are few jobs now where selling skills do not play a part in personal success, even where there is no direct customer-facing role.

The need for a competent, professional approach to sales is a key part of achieving competitive advantage both in industry and even not-for-profit organisations. As business processes and supply chains become more complex so the importance of an effective function becomes more appreciated. At the same time the fast growing small company sector sees owner-managers and directors whose main focus is on expanding sales for their business.

In the Institute of Professional Sales we work to provide lifelong support for sales staff and managers throughout their careers. Training and setting standards of competence are fundamental to the image of the profession. IPS also oversees continuous professional development and encourages networking. By creating a 'virtual spiral' of skills and competence we aim to raise the game in sales practice and win respect and recognition for the sales role.

Patrick Forsyth's book is an important milestone in the evolution of the sales profession, and a vital tool to help people who are either contemplating a career in sales or who recognise selling as one of the most useful paths to a top job in industry.

Michael Warne, Chief Executive, The Institute of Professional Sales

Acknowledgements

Writing a book such as this has only been possible because of the experience I have had working as a business developer myself. So thanks are due to many people I have met along the way, and in some cases with whom I remain in contact. Our crossing paths have provided – wittingly or otherwise – material and examples that I have drawn on and which are reflected in these pages. This certainly includes numbers of my clients: selling to them and working with them has also given me useful experience.

Specific thanks are due to a number of people at the Chartered Institute of Marketing. As a member of many years I suppose I expected certain assistance to be available, but what was provided went well beyond expectation and proved most useful. I spent time in their library, and discussed many aspects of marketing careers and education with members of their executive staff. Thanks are due therefore to their Corporate Marketing Manager, David Wright, and other members of his team including Ian Freeman. Similarly I would mention The Institute of Professional Sales, which also supplied information. I am especially grateful for permission to quote from several of both these institutes' brochures and publications; these are mentioned individually within the text and include in some cases a recommendation that readers consider acquiring the text.

Special thanks to Michael Warne, Chief Executive of The Institute of Professional Sales, for kindly contributing the Foreword.

This is the second book in this series I have written. The first, *Getting a Top Job in Marketing,* was one of those that launched the series. Sales and business development being a part of marketing I have drawn on that volume in writing this and there is thus a little overlap between the two books.

Finally, a word of thanks to publishers Kogan Page. I have written on various aspects of marketing in the past, but the idea for this series was very much their initiative. I am grateful to Philip Mudd for introducing the idea to me and for his support along the way as writing, production and launch of both my titles in the series progressed. This was welcome, helpful and also typical of the editorial team at Kogan Page, a number of whose members I have been pleased to work with in the past.

Introduction

Success is getting what you want.
Happiness is liking what you get.

H Jackson Brown

So you think you can find, develop and build business. You are serious about it too (well you are reading this!) Good. Sales and business development is a vital part of the marketing of any enterprise. It is also a challenging area, and an exciting and rewarding one in which to work. It is worthwhile too. Marketing is the business function that drives business to achieve profit and growth, whatever else it may involve, and it is a multifaceted activity – it would fail without a strong sales element.

Marketing needs all the talent it can get. Can you succeed in this most personal area of the marketing world? Well, why not? Certainly if you have the right characteristics, develop the appropriate skills, obtain the necessary qualifications, go about things in the right way and... but we are getting ahead of ourselves. You may just have a germ of an idea about a career in sales or marketing, you may have short-listed it as one of a number of possible careers, or you may already be working in it or near it and be wanting to make sure it treats you well. Whatever your situation, this book is intended to provide practical help. Specifically it is designed to:

▌ demystify business development and sales, and explain exactly what they are;
▌ set out the range of career possibilities that exist;
▌ give a flavour of what it is actually like to work in this area;
▌ provide guidelines on the way to proceed in order to get in, get on – and get to the top.

Again, whatever stage you are currently at, it is advantageous to look ahead – in this case towards a career in sales and business development – with a healthy respect for the realities of the world of work as it is now, and in light of the trends that will affect it in the future. Because of this, there are a number of other factors we will touch on along the way. These include:

▍ deciding what you want from your working life, assessing the situation and matching your needs to the realities of the job market;

▍ active approaches to career development, indeed career management, made ever more necessary by a changing world;

▍ focusing on the wide range of opportunities that exist in this area of corporate life with a view to short-listing the best area for you and the best career route to take;

▍ looking at the concept of the 'top job' in the context of the range of activity encompassed by sales. In fact, there are a variety of 'tops' and numbers of ways of getting to them.

The way ahead

The book's organisation reflects these factors. We start with this overview and introduction. Then, Chapter 1 adds an explanation designed to expose sales and business development in all its guises. Chapter 2 reviews the breadth of opportunities that exist in different job roles and in organisations marketing and selling different types of product and service.

We then turn to the jobs involved more specifically: to the range of different jobs it is possible to undertake in this area (Chapter 3), and the role of business development and how it extends the definition of selling (Chapter 4). Next, Chapter 5 offers guidance on how what is being sold affects jobs and careers, and Chapter 6 looks at the sales aspect involved in many senior and management jobs. An international flavour is added in Chapter 7 for those who see the world as their market. Then – because it is both topical and important – the area of e-commerce has its own chapter (8), which draws to some extent on a chapter in my book *Sales Management* (in Capstone Publishing's *ExpressExec* series). In

Chapter 9 the key skills and qualifications necessary for the career are reviewed, as are the techniques that must be deployed by sales people.

The final two chapters, 10 and 11, look at how to plan and manage such a career and where to find sales and business development jobs. Finally, a short reference section adds names and addresses of useful points of contact, ranging from management institutes to magazines, followed by a glossary.

Though the objective is to give a full picture of the opportunities that exist here, there is doubtless more to be said. This is not a book about how to undertake a selling role and, as will quickly become clear, this is a broad and important part of the marketing mix. Hence, perhaps a final objective is to prompt the reader to further investigation. If you are serious about this kind of career or about using it as a stepping-stone into other areas of business, particularly marketing, then time spent studying what is involved, how it works and how you can succeed in it is well worthwhile. This book is intended to provide a worthwhile start to that process, being valuable whatever stage of your career you are at.

This is an objective review. But – let me declare my prejudice – it is one that unashamedly reflects my personal enthusiasm for sales and business development and for the marketing activity of which it is part. I hope this enthusiasm may prove infectious, for I do believe that beyond it being a worthwhile and satisfying area of work – it is also fun.

Patrick Forsyth
Touchstone Training & Consultancy
28 Saltcote Maltings
Maldon
Essex CM9 4QP
Spring 2002

Note: What is sold may, of course, be a product or a service. In this book, where the difference is important each may be mentioned specifically, otherwise 'product' should be taken to mean 'product or service'.

Top task boxes

One purpose of this book is to give a flavour not only of what this area of sales and business development in all its manifestations is, but also what it is like to work in it. To this end a number of short, boxed sections appear throughout the text under the heading 'Top tasks'. These give snapshots of some of the tasks that work in this area can necessitate, and an indication of some of the areas which you might find questions or discussions focusing on in job interviews. The topics chosen range across the main areas reviewed here. They are not intended to be comprehensive or to put any order of priority on the examples used; they are to add something of a flavour of what working in sales is all about. They start here.

Top tasks
Maximising the opportunity

You are employed by a major international airline and amongst your customers are large corporate travel agents. These need calling on regularly to update them on the changing services and schedules of the airline and persuade them to recommend your flights. They are characterised by employing large numbers of staff all of whom may take an enquiry – for example, someone saying 'I need to arrange a flight to Hong Kong' – that puts them in a position to sell your particular flights.

The problem is to find a way of maximising the effectiveness of your visits. Specifically, you want to put your points across not just to the manager (for him or her to relay on to the staff) but to *all the staff who handle customer enquiries and reservations* (or, realistically, to as many of them as possible). Is there a way of doing this? Preferably one that will not just create a communication opportunity but also act to differentiate you from your competitors?

Note: this example is revisited in the next chapter and one real-life approach is quoted as an example.

---

1 Selling and business development defined

Any business needs customers; they earn their living in the marketplace. Customers need to be identified, attracted, interested and persuaded to buy. Doing this is, in an overall sense, the role of marketing. The word 'marketing' encompasses a number of things from the concept of giving customers what they want to the marketing mix (the four Ps: product, price, presentation and place). This is not the place to examine the many facets of marketing in detail, suffice to say that it constitutes the overall process that 'brings in the business'; the key essentials are shown in Figure 1.1. (For a clear overview of marketing and all that it entails see my books *Getting a Top Job in Marketing* or *Everything You Need to Know About Marketing*, both also Kogan Page paperbacks.)

This shows a cycle of activity, one that the marketing plan must specify in its entirety. It is a continuous process and, on the left-hand side of the figure, it is clear that selling is one of a number of different tactical techniques that can be deployed, in different mixes, to interface persuasively with potential customers. Indeed selling is different to all the other techniques – advertising, public relations, sales promotion and the rest – involving as it does personal, one-to-one communication between the organisation and its customers. Sales people complete the chain of links between the two parties, in fact this link may be seen as completing the whole marketing process.

Even today the old question is sometimes asked about what the difference is between marketing and selling. There should be no confusion. They are wholly different things, although selling is one inherent component part of the whole, and larger, marketing process and of the marketing mix.

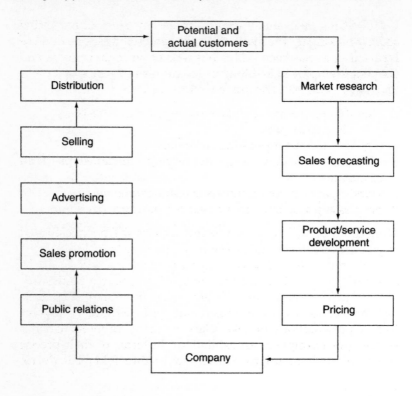

Figure 1.1   The marketing process

The role of selling

Whatever an organisation may do, producing products or services or even having some different overall aim (such as charity), it needs to tell people about it. The world will not automatically beat a path to its door: people need to be told it is there and attracted to it. An old saying, dating back to the advent of marketing, still makes a good point:

> They say if you build a better mousetrap than your neighbour, people are going to come running. They are like hell! It's marketing that makes the difference.
>
> *Ed Johnson*

This telling takes many forms – the many types of marketing activity making up the marketing mix – and selling is one of these forms. It is, as has been said, a business of personal contacts and the people employed in selling have a number of very specific jobs to do. Key amongst them are the following:

▌ identifying, qualifying and contacting new prospects;
▌ following up enquiries;
▌ regularly contacting existing customers;
▌ creating, managing and developing relationships with customers;
▌ working with major customers at a strategic level;
▌ progressing sales situations towards a purchase decision.

More could be added, indeed further aspects will be investigated as you read on. It should also be noted that the tasks listed above are not mutually exclusive factors. Overall the job could be summed up by saying that it is one consisting of communication. This in turn encompasses different things. For example contacts may be face-to-face, on the telephone, or in writing; or involve formal presentations or take place in many different circumstances (for example at an exhibition). In terms of their precise communication intentions, contacts have a threefold job to do, to:

1. inform;
2. persuade;
3. differentiate.

In today's competitive world all three are important. Certainly it is not sufficient only to say of a product, 'It's here' or to say how good it is – there are many 'good' products in most fields. The full message must tell people about it, make what is said persuasive and, more than that, make it seem better or more appropriate than other competitive offerings. Given the way even simple communication can cause problems, this is no easy job. Sales people need to be master communicators. They need to understand how and why people make decisions to buy and how to express themselves in a way that customers appreciate and take notice of – to the extent of taking action to buy.

The importance of selling

So, selling communicates with customers. That may not seem more than routine, but it is: it is much more than routine. Selling is literally the final link, sometimes in a chain of many links stretching over some considerable time, between an organisation and its customers. Consider the kind of progression of events that might be involved. The following is just an example; what actually occurs will vary with different kinds of business:

▌ *Advertising* (alerts a potential customer to the existence of something).

▌ *Press relations* (tells them more, perhaps pointing up some particular factor that rings bells with them).

▌ *Brochure* (they telephone the company for more information and printed information continues the persuasion).

▌ *Sales meeting* (either a sales person contacts them, following up their request for a brochure, or they take the initiative and contact the company – this results in a meeting with a sales person).

▌ *Further sales action* (the meeting may not tie things down, they might need a quotation, a written proposal or a formal presentation for their colleagues before a decision is made).

▌ *Follow up* (throughout the process additional contacts, perhaps by telephone, may be necessary to maintain a customer's interest).

▌ *Purchase* (at the end of this chain of events a decision is made – and the customer says Yes or No) and then a whole chain of action follows on, often either to continue persuasion or to prompt repeat business.

Such a process may take days, weeks or months (years where there is major expense or complexity). A plethora of communications may be involved in the early stages: a variety of advertisements are seen, the customer visits a trade show – there are many possibilities. In many businesses, although the broad contacts whet the appetite as it were, *only* the personal sales contact can convert initial interest into a firm order. Unless the sales person does his or her bit everything else is wasted. Advertising, for example, is expensive. It is, in effect, useless if the interest it creates in people is not successfully converted into business.

Furthermore what is being described is an essentially fragile process. The customer reserves the right to opt out at any stage. If the sales person does not conduct an effective meeting, the customer declines to go further and they never get a chance to write the brilliant proposal that might have clinched the deal. Every stage is important. Success only comes from the culmination of a series of individually successful stages being completed to the customer's satisfaction.

If the result is negative and the customer does not order (and sometimes it will be: no business has a 100 per cent strike rate), then the further through the cycle rejection occurs the more time has been wasted and the greater has been the cost. Conversely when the result is a sale then all the costs involved down the chain have paid their way.

So, is selling important? The answer must be that it is: very important. There is an old saying, 'Nothing happens until someone sells something.' In some organisations sales has no personal manifestation. This is true of a company in the catalogue business, for example. The catalogue lands on the doormat and customers send back the order form (though even here telephone sales staff may make a difference). There are other ways of operating that avoid the need for sales staff, but for most organisations the saying quoted above is literally true: without a sales resource – and one operating effectively – the business would not survive. If sales people make the difference between survival and going under, then surely their importance is not in doubt.

So far this description focuses sharply on the role of the classic field sales person. Other varieties of sales job – many others – are involved too. There are many categories of people with more individual and high profile sales jobs (titles such as Key Account Executive, National Accounts Manager abound), and we investigate these later. Managers in a variety of roles sell, including Managing Directors – selling remains a responsibility at high level in many fields and this is something else we will investigate in due course. There are also Sales Managers and Directors who oversee the operation of the people constituting the sales resource or sales team, whatever form that takes. All these people are important to the success of their organisations, and together they constitute a range of interesting and rewarding jobs and career paths.

Stereotyped images

Given the way the sales role is described above it is perhaps surprising that its image is sometimes – how can I put this? – less than high profile. Rarely in Europe will you hear people, when asked what they do, reply 'I sell' as you would to a greater extent in, say, the US. And for the layman the archetypal salesman is too often imagined to be a pushy spiv who drives a Ford Mondeo, is not to be trusted and sells double glazing or insurance. It is said of most people that if their daughter says she is to marry a double-glazing salesman their first response is to count the family silver, and their second is to lock it away!

How is it that such a valuable occupation should be typecast in this way? There are I think two reasons. There *are* some charlatans about. There are businesses that use sharp practice and there is a whole industry of television programmes and magazines telling us so (again this is something that we will touch on later, but it is not in this, thankfully small, area of the overall sales profession in which this book advocates there being career opportunities). More important, selling, like marketing, is seriously misunderstood. As part of the complexities of the marketing process this may be understandable to an extent – maybe marketing and sales people should do a better job of explaining what they do and why it is important.

Leaving the rogues to one side, when the true role of sales people is understood their importance can soon be appreciated. None of us likes to be sold what we do not need, but this is not what professional sales people do. It is a skilled job, one that contributes directly to organisational success and prosperity. One task of this book is to demonstrate just that. If you are at an early stage of formalising career plans, do not rule this one out until you have done sufficient checking to be judging the true picture.

The sales job day-to-day

Given its importance, what does all this say about the nature of the jobs involved in sales? The burden of the message here is that they can be interesting, exciting and rewarding. Sales jobs, at whatever level, are:

▌ Very much at the sharp end of organisational life; it is a role that needs to make things happen.
▌ Dynamic in nature: because markets are competitive and fast moving – as is competition – sales people are part of the organisation that must constantly keep up to date and amend the way they operate to be successful.
▌ Personal: although there are team elements involved, much sales work is conducted by an individual who must ultimately create his or her own success (though good companies provide direction and support).
▌ Exposed: given the personal nature of the role and what it must do, there is never any difficulty deciding whether someone has been successful. Sales results speak for themselves.

The job of communicating with people and of aiming to influence them is a constant challenge, as is the job of managing their time, territory and customer list for a member of a field sales team, or the job of negotiating with a major buyer for a Key Accounts Manager. Sales jobs allow a great deal of personal flexibility. They can be at – or act to get you to – the senior echelons of an organisation and they can supply a high level of job satisfaction as well as a good financial income. For those who find they have an affinity with jobs in the sales area, or with sales as part of their job, they can provide a satisfying career.

The link to top management

As has already been said, selling is an activity that takes place at various levels. You can be at the top of the sales ladder in an organisation. You can become top of the sales function, working to manage or direct a sales team as part of the overall management team involved in marketing. You can be a senior manager who has selling as a clear and important part of your portfolio of tasks (sometimes this may be in an organisation where only the senior people sell). Or you can deploy your sales skills for yourself, in your own business or on a freelance basis working on behalf of others. Sales has many links with the top, indeed there are many versions of just how we might define 'the top' in the sales area.

As we will see, what is described as 'sales' and as 'business development' overlap. On occasion, attempts are made to boost the image of sales by inventing fancy titles, but otherwise 'business development' tends to be used in certain industries (usually where they are dealing with major customers, and where what is sold commands a high price for a typical individual order). The distinction between the two will progressively become clearer as we move on, but the usage does not have the precision it might.

Conclusion

Sales may be misunderstood. It may encompass a mixed selection of different jobs. But it is certainly an important element of the way many organisations operate; without it working well their success would be limited or curtailed. It offers a career with interest and satisfaction at every level; and it offers both top jobs in its own right and a route to the top in a broader sense too.

Top tasks
Maximising the opportunity (continued)

In the Introduction we looked at a sales situation in a major international airline. (A common problem in this industry is the need to brief and update travel agents: not just the manager of such establishments, but all their staff who have customer contact and who might influence their customer's choice.)

In this organisation one particular salesman had evolved a well-proven approach to deal with this in major outlets in which the number of such people were greatest. He would arrive, by appointment, and with a tray of coffee and doughnuts bought at a nearby shop. He had persuaded his customer to allow him to convene an impromptu coffee break: a group of the staff gathered round and he had their undivided attention for 15 to

---

20 minutes. In a large outlet he would do this twice, or more, to accommodate all the staff yet prevent their service to customers from being decimated. It was a scheme that worked well for all concerned. It was also not easy to copy: possession is nine points of the law and he had set a precedent – you cannot have that many coffee breaks in the same morning and competitors found it difficult to deal with the situation in a way that was as productive for them.

This seems like precisely the sort of good thinking that should be endemic around a sales operation. It worked well because it took account of the needs of the customer and did not seek simply to achieve what the sales side wanted. If such an idea suits even a small number of customers it is worthwhile (and different solutions must be sought with others).

This is certainly the sort of idea that can be developed by one person and then the experience can be circulated so that others in the organisation can try it too. This example provides one small snapshot to continue to build a picture of what sales work is like.

2 The range of opportunities

Opportunities are only opportunities if you know that they exist. In such a broad and disparate field as sales and business development, there is certainly a danger that a lack of understanding about just how much it encompasses can act to obscure potential opportunities. Hence the need to review the field (and for a book such as this) ahead of making any decisions about whether this is the career for you and, if so, where within it you want to be.

Early on in life, your background and circumstances colour your breadth of vision. One example links two points here. My father was a dentist; a perfectly good and necessary occupation. What is more, it is probably an occupation that people understand (they may not like it, but they understand it!). All dentists essentially do the same job and fix people's teeth. The first point this highlights is that this is not the case with many jobs in sales and marketing: in many circles there is no similar easy understanding of their role or what it entails. If something about it intrigues you, you need to find out more, to discover exactly what it in fact involves, and where within it you might find a desirable career.

Secondly, your career choice may be influenced by your current knowledge. Brought up in a small town where my father moved primarily in medical and professional circles, I knew little of the business world until the need for career choice prompted some investigation (though I did know I did not want to be a dentist).

Too much choice?

The complex modern world offers many career choices, even though adopting many of them is dependent on acquiring certain skills or qualifications. In my case, even if I could have obtained the various qualifications needed to become a dentist, my natural tendency towards hamfistedness would have ruled it out as suitable work. The sheer range of possibilities may make choice difficult. What is needed is a process of reducing the range of options, focusing on a narrower and narrower list until a final choice becomes clear. Complete career guidance is beyond our brief here. However, once you are at the point of identifying that your future lies in a 'business' career (whether the kind of organisation you see as a potential employer is to be commercial or not), and that sales, and perhaps marketing, is the area you wish to pursue, then the following thoughts may assist your further decision making.

Striking a balance

Any decision to pursue a particular career course needs to incorporate and balance two approaches. The first is the _practical:_ you need to consider what is possible. In some careers there are basic physical criteria that dictate whether you can go into something. A simple example is being above the minimum height to go into the police. Similarly you need to consider whether it is practical for you to add any necessary abilities which a particular course might make necessary: fluency in a foreign language for instance. Practical considerations range wide, from the ease or otherwise of getting into a narrow field of activity, however well suited you are for it, to the working hours that it entails and your ability to work in that way.

The second approach is the _desirable:_ you need to consider alongside the practical what you really _want_, and how much you want it. You may be prepared to move heaven and earth to achieve your aims, to set your sights high and compromise little or not at all.

For most people there must be a degree of compromise here – though you should take a considered view of things. Many people manage to get nearer their ideal than they at one time dared to hope – perseverance can be a powerful influence. A practical view _is_ important, but too much compromise might be regretted for a long time. The moral is to balance the two factors very carefully, and set objectives accordingly.

15

A view of qualifications

For many career choices a formal qualification is simply a necessity. This may be the case in technical fields, for example. For other jobs too a qualification may be necessary: we have all seen job advertisements stating 'graduates only' or similar, but just what it is remains more open. Other career paths are simply made easier to pursue if you are well qualified. Remember careers are essentially competitive and an employer faced with two similar candidates may make decisions partly on a rule of thumb basis, pursuing whoever has the 'best qualifications'.

Qualifications are reviewed in more detail in Chapter 9. Here it is only sought to highlight their role in creating opportunities and extending choice. In this context, certain other points are worth a word or two:

▌ *Immediate impact:* a qualification may open doors at once, making a particular job application possible soon after the qualification is awarded.
▌ *Lasting power:* as you move along a particular career path, it can be that the experience you accumulate becomes more important in assisting your progress than an earlier acquired qualification (especially the more general ones). But equally this may not be the case, and you could find yourself blessing the day you completed a course even many years after it was done.
▌ *Perceptions:* it is worth noting also that a qualification does not always produce a precise and specific effect – with an MBA in Marketing scoring nine out of ten, say. The perception others have of what you have achieved is equally important. For example, an employer may be as much impressed by the perseverance shown by your doing something in difficult circumstances as by the qualification it gave you. Or they may be influenced by the precise course you opted for and where you went to do it, as much as what it was.

There is, however, a direct relationship between qualifications and the range of options you will be able to consider. It is certainly still possible to succeed in sales and business development with little or nothing in the way of formal qualifications, but choice is equally certainly likely to be reduced. More important perhaps, although this is an area into which you might get without many or high qualifications, the lack of them may make upward progress thereafter more difficult. Your decisions about how far to take things and what particular qualifications to take and when, where and how to undertake them, need considering in this light. As a general rule it is often said that it is better to aim to become well qualified, but there is no one fixed situation to consider here. If you want to be a doctor, say, then certain qualifications are mandatory. Without such a cut-and-dried situation to contemplate, those going into these kinds of areas must form a considered view in light of what they want to achieve in future. We return to this anon.

The ways forward

It is perhaps an attractive feature of working in sales and business development that it offers no single clearly defined career path. There are some logical progressions, for example:

▎ Inside sales support roles (including telephone selling and even call centre work) can lead to field sales jobs.
▎ Basic field sales jobs can lead to more senior level sales appointments.
▎ Any sales job might lead on to sales management (ultimately becoming Sales Director, perhaps).
▎ Sales, or sales management, may lead into marketing (or other areas of managing people).
▎ Sales experience can lead into a wide variety of management roles where the need to sell is a part of the work portfolio.

That said, all sorts of routes are feasible. It is perfectly possible to go straight into a sales job and move on from there. Alternatively, large companies may recruit graduates into planned traineeships. Such typically put people through a progression that takes in a number of marketing functions – including sales. Here there is an opportunity to explore the potential exhibited in each before aiming someone along a particular path (preferably with their active participation). In other circumstances, progress may 'happen' more from serendipity and planning 'as you go'. For example, computer skills may take someone into the technical side of an IT company, but communications skills, say, provide a platform for movement into sales. Such non-standard progress can be as actively worked at as any other, of course.

In all cases, it makes progress more certain if you have clear objectives and aim actively to manage the development of your career. This is an area investigated further in Chapter 10. I do not want to favour either more conventional or contrived pathways here. Both are possible, though both must be approached practically and all need working at if the chances of success are to be increased.

A basis for decision

By its nature, sales and business development offers a range of job and career options. A variety of different factors need to be considered in forming a decision and making a choice. These include:

▌ You, your character, likes, dislikes and skills and qualifications.
▌ The precise role within the overall sales area that you see as attractive.
▌ The actual job you want to do (eg, Key Accounts Executive or Sales Manager).
▌ The product or service that an organisation markets (and thus the industry it is within).
▌ The size, and thus nature, of organisation that will be your employer.
▌ The markets you will be involved in (eg, industrial or consumer, national or international) and thus the kinds of customer situation involved.

There is a good deal to contemplate; an informed and considered decision is usually best, and these areas of decision and more are touched on further in the remaining pages.

One thing should be clear at this stage: not only are interesting, exciting and worthwhile career choices on offer here, but there are options that can appeal to a wide spectrum of people because of the plethora of different job choices offered. There is certainly no lack of opportunities for anyone suitable looking at the sales area; indeed many would say that this is an area of business that needs all the talent that it can attract.

A key question – rewards

Before we move on from a review of the opportunities these areas offer, it is perhaps a good idea to address the question of rewards (unless you seek no remuneration for your work!)

Clearly pay varies depending on a number of factors such as size of employer and the precise role within its marketing mix that a particular job entails. For instance, consider someone in a top job in a specialised area such as key account management. Especially in an area where such a role is very important (as with many consumer goods products), he or she might well earn more than a Marketing Manager in certain other kinds of organisation, for example a smaller firm.

Given the range and scope involved here there is some complexity of comparisons like this that one could make. Any specific figures quoted would, of course, quickly date. However, it's safe to say that overall salaries can compare well with other jobs in the organisational world. While reward levels change all the time, it is possible to check the state of play (pay!) and the trends.

The main overall source to check is _The Marketing Rewards Survey_ compiled annually by The Chartered Institute of Marketing (in association with the Rewards Group). This is available for purchase, though it is quite expensive. You may find a copy of it in a business library, or the summary published in the Institute's magazine _Marketing Business_ may give you sufficient information. For sales people specifically, the range is wide – for example a survey, _The Future of Selling_, produced by Quest Media, the publishers of _Winning Business_ (the prime journal for sales management) showed recently that the top sales people earned 44 per cent more than those at lower levels. Other factors play a part too. These include the industry chosen (for example many technical areas are high payers), whether commission is part of the package (often it is; this may make for a higher total return but more risk), and what the total package incorporates. Jobs involving a high proportion of commission payment can provide very high remuneration for some people.

As with any job, the careerist should be as much concerned about the package as the immediate salary, and remember that a wide range of perks are used to augment packages. If you are young, do not ignore things like pensions (they will matter soon enough!) Remember too that sales jobs are more likely to involve rewards that link to results than many other aspects of business. Some of these rewards may come in the form of things like share options that do not pay the mortgage from day one, but which can be worth a significant amount in the longer term.

The sales area has much to offer, and that includes the financial return as well as the satisfactions. With that in mind we turn to further factors affecting career choice; in the next chapter we consider the many different types of sales job that exist.

3 The many kinds of sales job

To prompt customer commitment and secure orders, the marketing process must end with personal contact in many kinds of organisation. Just what this is, and the form it takes, varies. Certainly, from the point of view of the people doing the job, one factor that creates differences is the product or service being sold – and thus the kind of customer with whom communication is necessary. This factor may make for radical differences. One person may, in financial services, spend his or her time discussing investments and pension arrangements with people in their own homes. Another, selling mining equipment, may spend some of his or her time a mile underground wearing overalls and a hard hat and talking to engineers.

The question of how the product being sold affects things is discussed in Chapter 5; here we look at things from the point of view of the organisation and its marketing activity and see what various sales methodologies and roles their strategy creates. There are opportunities throughout the piece.

A sales role

All sorts of people sell. Retail staff form one category of sales person and those wanting a career in retail marketing may find a spell doing this provides useful experience. The waiter who says, 'Another drink?' is selling; the air-hostess saying, 'Duty free?' is selling, even the manager in the building society who says, 'This is the best form of mortgage for you' is selling. These examples are mentioned only to make clear the wide application of persuasive skills. Here we focus on those jobs more readily conjured up by the description 'sales person'; there are still a whole range of different categories.

Horses for courses

The following illustrates the main categories. There is some overlap here, but no matter, the idea is to illustrate how the sales resource is deployed, not to be pedantic about drawing lines.

Inside sales

This is a category that includes staff in sales offices, which may be large or small. The staff undertake a mixture of tasks: handling enquiries, taking orders, following up contacts and sorting out queries as well as sometimes having a more active outgoing role in initiating contact with new or existing contacts. Contact is primarily by telephone, post, fax and e-mail rather than face-to-face.

At the other end of the spectrum there are sophisticated call centres (such as have become a feature of banking or insurance sales). Top jobs in specialised areas here can pay well and all such operations need people in management roles to organise and maintain the operation. The term 'sales support staff' is sometimes used here.

Telephone sales

There is certainly some overlap here with the first category, but some people work in a role concerned exclusively with telephone contact. This may be a first stage in the sales process: setting up appointments for full sales meetings for instance. It may involve high volumes of cold calling and a low strike rate at best. Often an element of commission is involved in the payment of people in this role, indeed it is one of a comparatively small number of fields where it is common to find commission-only as the basis for pay. Again, management posts are involved here and it can act as a stepping-stone to other kinds of sales job.

Van sales

This is somewhat low level selling, but again may lead to other things. The term describes those who sell and deliver in one operation (this may be shops – as with bread, or to businesses – as with fuel oil, or to homes – as with fresh fish).

Door-to-door

There are still plenty of things sold house-to-house and to items traditionally sold this way, such as encyclopaedias, have been added many new ones, for instance electricity and gas. This may not be everyone's cup of tea as a job, but again it can be a stepping-stone. Perhaps other kinds of selling such as home parties, the technique pioneered by Tupperware and now used by others ranging from children's books to lingerie, might logically be included here.

Missionary selling

This term is used when the sales person is unable to obtain an order in any direct manner, and where this occurs because of the nature of the business in question. Examples include those selling pharmaceutical products to doctors, representatives of breweries, certain situations in publishing (selling to universities in order to get a book put on a recommended reading list). This applies particularly where the contact is a specifier, that is someone like an architect or an accountant (the latter will only prompt the purchase of, say, a software package when they have a client needing it). This is also sometimes called 'goodwill selling'.

Commodity selling

The term is not used here in the financial sense, but of products without great differentiation. The sales process may be fairly standard, but the nature of the product puts more emphasis on the person selling themselves, being ultra reliable, and creating enough difference for the buyer to favour them over others. Products viewed in this way include such things as sand and cement sold to the building trade, basic chemicals used in manufacturing, etc. It also includes commodities such as electricity, now that markets have been opened and there is no monopoly supplier.

Group selling

This slightly less common term describes those who sell to groups, a buying situation where the 'decision maker' is not one but several people – a committee, the board of directors, or a project team. This can apply in fields as diverse as defence equipment or corporate banking.

Different categories

There is a major division between two contrasting categories. The first is *retail sales people,* or rather those people selling to retailers. Here, of course, the product is for resale. Jobs here vary too. In the food trade in the UK some 80 per cent of food products go through just five major groups (Tesco, etc) and the job to be done is rather different to the job of selling to small retailers. The profusion of different types of retailer is bewildering, from the corner shop to supermarkets, out-of-town shopping centres and department stores. Shops may be highly specialised, like TieRack, and sell one product or a tightly focused range, or may sell many things. They may be large or small. All need regular contact. This is a major area of selling, so many companies are involved and there are also plenty of management opportunities in this area. Though the price of individual products may be low, the volume makes this a major area of business and influences the rewards.

Top tasks
Have I got you where you want me?

You are Key Accounts Manager for a major packaged food company dealing regularly with one of the big supermarket chains, one that controls some 15 per cent of your market. It buys and stocks your product and achieves reasonable volumes with it. You have been trying to get it to increase the visibility of your product, devoting more space to its display and linking this to various promotional offers directed at the consumer. The company asks to see you – an extra meeting. You can guess what it is about. It wants to negotiate. It is after greater margin from you in return for some sort of additional promotional support.

You want the extra publicity, you want to maintain good relations with the company, but you also want to preserve margins as much as possible. Can you negotiate and secure a good deal?

The second is *industrial selling*: here sales people call on other businesses. A tyre manufacturer must sell to all the car manufacturers to compete for sales of tyres being used as original equipment, for example. People here are also referred to as 'technical sales people' or 'sales engineers', and many highly technical products are involved, from a machine tool to an airliner. Many jobs here demand a technical bent or qualification, many of the major – and thus expensive – products involved give rise to senior jobs and high salaries. This area overlaps with what, more recently, has tended to be called 'business-to-business selling' (mainly used to describe simpler products sold this way – office furniture, perhaps, rather than power stations). In addition, specific sectors have acquired their own special terminology. For example SOHO stands for Small office/Home office and is used to categorise that growing market. Those working in the sector would perhaps be described as SOHO sales people.

Although there is a danger of compounding the overlaps, we might consider one more category and separate those selling *intangibles* like advertising space or investments from the area of *products*. There is a part of the service, rather than product category that needs a particularly creative approach and sometimes you will see the term 'speciality' or 'creative speciality' used to describe such areas of sales activity. Lastly, working in export or internationally may expand this list (this is explored in Chapter 7).

Some people make their career in one sector, others move from one to another, expanding their experience and moving up the ladder. Others too may be in one particular type of selling simply because it goes with the kind of product they want to sell or the kind of organisation they want to be involved with.

The core field role

In days prior to this era of political correctness one used to talk about a 'salesman'. This term defined the sales job of a member of a field sales team, as opposed to sales people doing other sorts of job (such as the retail assistant). Now we have to use three words – field sales person – to focus on this core category. 'Representative', or 'rep' has become old fashioned and seems not to describe someone deploying the professional approach that selling now demands, though it is still used, with perfectly professional connotations, in some industries, including publishing.

Top tasks
Falling on stony ground

You are calling on a regular customer. You get on well. Your track record with them individually and as an organisation is good. Nevertheless you are prepared, you have thought through your approach and, from experience, have no reason to expect other than a welcome.

This time, almost before you have said 'Hello' there is an angry outburst. 'Do you know what happened with that last delivery? Late? It was hardly in the right month! It is just not good enough and I am still waiting for an apology from the idiot I spoke to in your office....'

A major complaint threatens to derail your plans and seems to threaten your whole relationship with the customer. Literally the next few words you say can start to retrieve the situation or dig the hole deeper, possibly so deep that escape is impossible – you have barely a couple of seconds to collect your thoughts. What do you say and what approach to solving the problem should it lead into?

Whatever the name, let us focus on this core job for a moment. Field sales people do a variety of different jobs as has been described above, but some factors are common. They are rightly thought of as managers of a territory. Often this is a geographic area (for example, Kent and Sussex), but it might rather be industry based, calling on one particular kind of buyer (eg, people in one industrial sector). Sometimes both things are combined in a matrix of organisation. Sometimes linking product specialisation into the picture further complicates the arrangement.

All such people are responsible for managing:

▌ their time (bearing in mind that they are away from the office for most of it);
▌ their customers (numbering from just a few to many hundreds, depending on the industry);
▌ the productivity of their working (for example, dealing with administration so that it is kept effective and under control and maximising the amount of time they spend face-to-face with customers).

It is common for sales people to spend only 20 to 30 per cent of their working time with customers. This may sound a failure and you might well ask, 'What are they doing for the rest of the time?' Admin takes up some of it. Waiting takes up more and travel is a major component (and the roads seem to get worse all the time); in addition you have to take into account a variety of things from attending sales meetings, training, sick leave and holidays. _Sales productivity_ is therefore a major issue both at sales person and at management levels.

The job involves a number of aspects:

▌ Organising the way a territory is worked.
▌ Planning for individual calls to make sure that their effectiveness is maximised.
▌ Making those calls – and making the most of them.
▌ Creating, maintaining and developing good business relationships with customers.
▌ Servicing the customer base (there often being an overlap between sales and service).
▌ Communicating to maintain contact between face-to-face visits (in writing, by telephone, whatever).

▌ Fire-fighting (even in the tightest ship there may be occasional problems, such as customer complaints).

▌ Backing up this activity with appropriate record keeping and administration.

▌ Liaison with others around the organisation as necessary (eg, a technical department).

Beyond that, sales people may spend time at sales meetings, in training and dealing with other more corporate matters. An important additional factor for many is feedback. Sales people have far more customer contact than virtually anyone else in the organisation, and their ability to feed back front line information, make suggestions for building business, changing products, combating competition, etc is – or should be – legion. There is every reason for their role to be seen as creative and for them to make a contribution that goes beyond managing their discreet territory.

Customers are more and more demanding. They have increasingly high expectations, low loyalty to their existing suppliers and become more fickle in every way every day. The job described is a challenging one. The opportunity to maximise the potential from the market by maximising the effectiveness of the sales role is considerable. The proper functioning of the sales resource is a variable and differentiating factor, one that can give an organisation an edge over its competitors. It demands a professional approach and it demands considerable skill. What is more the skills it does demand need constant updating. More of this aspect is commented on in Chapter 9.

There are two further areas to consider here to produce a more rounded picture; these are picked up under the next two headings.

Special tasks

In addition to the overall task described above, other tasks may be involved with specific product and industrial areas. These include:

▌ *Prospecting:* a proportion of the total time may need to be deployed in identifying and approaching – cold calling – new prospects as well as looking after existing ones (or following up 'warm' ones in the form of enquiries received).

▊ *Demonstration*: with certain products customers demand to see them in action or to try them out. Whether this involves a car being taken for a test drive, an office machine being demonstrated at someone's desk side, or an elaborate test of a new factory system – it adds a special dimension to the core sales job. There is only one way to conduct demonstrations: everything must go 100 per cent right. Customers will put up with no less and will quickly conclude, 'If they cannot make it work, what hope for me', if everything does not go smoothly.

▊ *Presentation*: communication must be clear and persuasive one-to-one, but sometimes there is a need for formal presentations, such as speaking to a group (eg, a buying committee); this links to skills, see below.

▊ *Analysis:* sales people have to be able to plan a strategy regarding the ongoing relationship with customers, especially with large ones. Remember that as a general rule Pareto's Law applies here (the 80/20 rule) and that 80 per cent of sales revenue will come from 20 per cent of an organisation's customers: the larger ones. This means analysing situations, including past results, and creating an ongoing future action plan that works, and is the best way of maximising sales potential given the realities.

▊ *Dealing with special circumstances*: some selling may take place in exceptional circumstances. One example of this, used by many companies, is exhibitions, trade shows, etc. Staffed by the sales team, these are events that demand a rather different approach to the individual sales meeting. They are also expensive, so every contact made must go well. Taking one step forward and saying, 'Can I help you?' (to which the retort is usually 'No') is not enough. In some industries certain events are crucial: they are the only way of accessing particular kinds of business. If this book ever appears in any foreign languages, then it will almost certainly be because someone at Kogan Page knows how to conduct themselves at the annual worldwide publishing event – the Frankfurt Book Fair – where the majority of such deals are struck.

These make good examples, but the list could be extended. Some businesses use very particular methods: for example someone selling financial services could find him or herself working to a large extent off a laptop computer (which enhances their presentation – and its heavily regulated precision – with suitable graphics). Someone selling farm machinery may spend most of his or her time in the open air, wearing wellington boots, and conducting a sales meeting with farmers seemingly impervious to the smells around them. Some jobs may include many or most of these tasks.

Special skills

The core task demands that people can communicate effectively and persuasively. Just ensuring clear understanding alone is no easy matter; think how easy it is to get at cross-purposes with someone even when the communication is straightforward and no persuasion is involved. This should not be underestimated.

Other skills may be necessary too. This theme is picked up in Chapter 9, but suffice to say here that they include such things as numeracy, computer literacy, negotiation and business writing.

Never listen to anyone who denigrates sales jobs: they may seem deceptively simple – demanding only the gift of the gab – but they are not. It is a job that demands particular talents and skills and a great deal hangs on their effective deployment.

Different reward systems

There is a range of different reward systems for sales jobs. The extremes are easy to describe: the straight salary and no salary at all, with payment solely on results in the form of commission. Research shows that sales people tend to perform best when there is an element of commission, so probably the majority of jobs do have this. Two factors should be noted here.

First, it must be possible to pay commission. This needs to be done on a reasonable lead-time and reflect the work of an individual. In some businesses, where a team works together and long lead times are involved this may simply not be possible. Second, payment by results means just that: no results – no pay (or none of the element that comes from results). There is an equation, albeit an imprecise one, that relates commission and risk. High commission jobs may be inherently more risky, but this is not necessarily a bad thing and for those who are successful and thrive in this environment, the rewards may be great. (The fact that if lots of people buy this book the royalties I receive will be greater is a similar principle; but I digress.)

Most jobs therefore offer a mix of salary and commission and there are other elements too that deserve thinking about. A high proportion of sales jobs involve someone travelling, and thus offer their incumbents a company car. There may well be other things that are some kind of 'perk' forming part of a package, for example a laptop computer or mobile telephone that is available for private use. One caveat here: benefits in kind are often taxed and, in the UK at least, the tax on company cars is becoming somewhat draconian. This needs watching in assessing potential rewards and the best deal.

Sales jobs are often rewarded in part with reference to results and this is true at levels right to the top. Senior people may have profit-sharing schemes, instead of commission, to tie them into the overall success of the organisation. There are also a variety of share schemes that can involve people by giving them a stake in the company.

Beyond the considerations mentioned, as with any job in fact, the package for sales positions should be looked at in the round and a balanced view taken of it – for example between high commission in the short term and less ideal pension provision than you might like.

Hard sell and rogues

A word is due in a book like this about the less ethical side of selling, which doubtless exists. Some areas of business are unethical or even illegal, and whatever the potential rewards of ripping off old ladies by selling them, say, home insulation of some sort, it will not find recommendation here as a field in which to seek a career.

There are categories of sales activity that can have a dubious reputation, and may indeed sail close to the wind on occasions, but which do also hold out real and acceptable opportunities for some people. I must be circumspect in suggesting examples. But one that might come to many people's minds is time shares (in the holiday and holiday property sense). Clearly there has been illegal and questionable activity in this area. Perhaps sales people have been ripped off as well as customers, but there are also some – maybe one should say many – operations that are well run, whose customers are content and where there are good and rewarding opportunities for those employed there in sales roles.

The moral is clear. If you see opportunities in such an area, always be circumspect. Check them out and consider the longer term as well as the short. It would be wrong to write off a whole industry from your consideration because it seems unsavoury, but equally there are dangers in proceeding toward something that needs careful checking without actually doing it.

Looking ahead

In so dynamic an area it seems appropriate to look ahead. *The Future of Selling* is a report published late in 2000 by Quest Media Ltd (the publishers of the journal *Winning Business*). Produced in association with the Institute of Professional Sales and consultants Miller Heiman Inc, it is directed towards sales managers and directors. It is an interesting research study, more so because the area is so rarely researched. It reviews current practice and looks to the future, examining the changing sales role, customer expectations and beliefs, and the whole way sales teams are organised, staffed, rewarded and managed. Key findings indicated that:

▌ Customers are becoming better informed and more organised, demanding and sharp in their dealings with sales people (with the Internet being used to a significant extent for pre-buying research).
▌ Technology is having, and will continue to have an effect on sales activity: most dramatically it is replacing sales people with electronic, impersonal buying, though this is not affecting large numbers of business areas. The dynamic nature of this area is evidenced by the uncertainty respondents reflected in their forecasts of what other influences are becoming important.

▌ Recruitment is a perpetual challenge, as is retention.

▌ CRM (customer relationship marketing) is becoming a more widespread basis for many customer interactions, and creating a more formal basis for them.

▌ Training remains a constant need (and more of it is being done, and the range of ways in which it is done is also widening) as the level of competency of sales people is seen as key to success.

▌ Reporting takes a high proportion of working time, reducing sales people's time spent face-to-face with customers; this despite the increasing computerisation of data collection and reporting systems.

Sales management, its practice, manner and style, is seen as significant to success. On the one hand the increasing professionalism of the sales role, and the broadening of sales people's responsibilities in response to market changes, heighten the role and managerial skills sales managers must have. On the other hand, there is one area where sales managers sometimes seem to be marginalized: new technology. For example, sales managers are often not involved in the development of e-business strategies. There may be dangers here: an e-business strategy that is not made compatible with traditional sales processes may lack realism. While technology and its development are always difficult to predict, it is surely best done in this area with the active involvement of the sales manager, or the baby might just get thrown out with the bath water. The section of the report on the impact of e-commerce is interesting. Just to quote one statistic: 90 per cent of respondents' organisations have a Web site; but 57 per cent of them said they were not used to assist sales.

Top tasks

Reassessment

For whatever reason, economic conditions are changing for the worse. Your buyers react by sharpening their approach. They talk to more people and take more time before making a decision (or put things off completely). They balk at prices

> more than usual and they want to negotiate more. They are
> more demanding over everything: quality and service in all
> their forms. Their loyalty to existing, trusted suppliers evapo-
> rates. You have to try to match their reaction and secure the
> maximum amount of business despite the changed conditions.
> What changes should you make to your own approach?

It is a valuable study that deserves to be repeated on a regular
basis. Perhaps it is something to track down if this is an area that
interests you.

Summary

The sales function lacks for nothing in the variety stakes, and as
we have seen above, variety is likely to increase with changing
circumstances. The field encompasses a wide range of different
jobs. It operates in practically every area of business and organisational endeavour, and there are people in what are effectively
sales roles in everything from charities (what else does a
fundraiser do, if not persuade?) to government departments and
other non-profit-making activities.

In addition to the picture painted so far, sales shades into
business development and that extends things a good bit further;
and we still have to review the links between selling and
management (both of these have chapters of their own). Next
though, business development warrants its own chapter.

4 *Business development*

Is business development just a grand term for selling, designed to make it sound more important? Well, yes and no. It is the case that the importance of many sales jobs is exaggerated by the way they are described, but business development has a real independent existence too. One useful way to look at the positioning of business development is shown graphically in Figure 4.1.

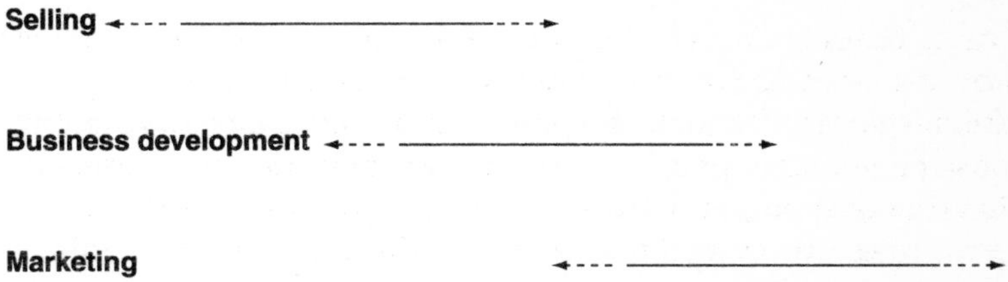

Selling ◄ - - - ──────────────── - - - ►

Business development ◄ - - - ──────────────── - - - ►

Marketing   ◄ - - - ──────────────── - - - ►

Figure 4.1   The interrelationship between selling, business development and marketing

In other words the activities overlap, there is no definitive border line between one and another, nor are certain activities discreet to just one of the three broad areas shown. For example, prospecting – activity to locate and contact new prospects – can be carried out in different ways in all three areas.

A complex process

Some kinds of selling seem, indeed are, comparatively simple processes. Sometimes a sales process may be completed in one single transaction. In my own case, for instance, I might meet a

man, perhaps in the course of other existing activity such as conducting a public training course. We talk and he agrees to me
conducting some training for him. It is not often so straightforward,
of course, (if only!) and what occurs in the one communication
must be right, but sometimes – and in some businesses – that is all
that is involved.

Now let us consider a more complex example and allow that to
lead us to a clearer explanation of the concept of business development. Imagine a company that makes a deceptively simple
product, like glass bottles. Seemingly a commodity product, they
end up lining the supermarket shelves in their millions. They
come in a variety of shapes and sizes and are filled with everything from beer to shampoo. They are also, from a marketing
standpoint, an inherent part of the product. They must protect,
standing up to the manufacturing and distribution process, as
well as use by the consumer. They represent a portion of total
product cost, and thus affect pricing policy. They are also an
inherent part of the presentation of the product, normally seen as
linked to quality and purity in a way that plastic or other materials
find difficult to mirror. They have even acquired an environmen-
tally friendly image in an age of recycling.

But how are they sold? First the bottle manufacturer has to
locate prospective customers. Let us assume that one such manu-
factures toiletries. It has a whole list of requirements as to what the
bottles it buys must be. Such criteria will include price, material
factors (weight, strength, ease of filling, etc) and design – the bottle
must add to the product's appeal and must help make the product
fly off the shelves. The company also wants a regular, reliable
supply: if it has no bottles then production grinds to an abrupt halt
and it can ship no shampoo. It may therefore not be prepared to
buy all its bottles from one supplier, feeling that this makes it
vulnerable. The task facing the sales people at the bottle manufacturer is thus a daunting one. They must sell the product in a
conventional sense, but with some prospects they almost certainly
will also have to get involved with design and how it aids their
customer's marketing. Perhaps they have to respond to a design
brief and persuade their potential customer that they can produce
a bottle with all the required characteristics and do so at the right
price and technical specification. Perhaps to make any headway

they must initiate design suggestions and come up with some new shapes and appearances.

To work in this way they need knowledge of the trade through which the product (shampoo) is sold, that is everything from pharmacies to supermarkets and hairdressers. After all if a design is not found attractive at that level, the product will not sell, and in turn their sales of bottles will decline or dry up. Even if they are successful, and supplies of bottles start to be ordered, then the liaison with all concerned must continue. More may be involved here too. If the shampoo manufacturer uses a contract bottling organisation (sending them bulk supplies of shampoo to actually put into bottles), then they too need contact – it is to them that deliveries will actually go, and any problems that the bottles cause on the bottling line will show up there first.

If repeat and continuous ordering is to occur, and if the business is to grow with a variety of bottle sizes and designs being ordered, and the total revenue thus increasing, then ongoing sales activity is necessary. The job – in terms of who does what, how they do it and the time it all takes – is complex. It may well go beyond sales too. For example, maybe such a firm would undertake market research: asking consumers – those who buy shampoo – about the packaging they like and choose. The information obtained could then be used by the sales people in their discussions, helping to enhance their effectiveness, and making their offering more attractive.

Even a snapshot like this of just one situation makes the point: some sales processes are far more than one transaction. Many industries and products could be described in this way, all having their own version of this kind of chain of events and elements. Those involved in such a process are likely to regard it as 'business development' rather than simply as 'selling'. At its heart the process must ensure selling occurs successfully, but much more than this is involved.

The characteristics of complex sales

Although there are great differences in detail between glass bottles and other products, there are also certain common elements that crop up where the process to be gone through is complex and thus better described as business development rather than as selling.

Contacts are at senior level

It is the perceived importance of the transaction in the customer's organisation that primarily dictates the levels at which discussions take place. In the example above, the bottle is so important to the company's shampoo sales that many people, including senior marketing or promotions people, are likely to be involved as well as those on the production side. Similarly, to take a completely different example, if a company is deciding which advertising agency is to be used it is a choice likely to be made at a senior level.

Top tasks
Follow up and persistence

You have been through a long series of contacts with a prospective customer, culminating in a meeting that seemed to go well – you were sure in your own mind that they would confirm an order. But at the end you were faced not with a 'Yes' or a 'No', but that great favourite (sic) of sales people everywhere: 'Leave it with me.' Despite your handling of the situation (there are techniques that can sometimes get round this classic sticking point) the outcome could not be changed.

You are also persistent and have followed up several times to try to discover what is going on and encourage the process back on track towards an order. You have telephoned, written and sent e-mails. The best you have got by way of reply is a secretary saying (more dreaded words), 'He's in a meeting.' Several weeks have gone by and today the file has popped out of your prompt system demanding that you follow up again.

It is time to think creatively. What can you do this time that is different and powerful enough to get a real answer and act to make it a positive one?

Time scale

Usually complexity goes with a long lead-time. For example, with many products such a process might well take weeks or months, and for some – say an aircraft or telecommunications system – it might take years. This makes the sales process exceptionally vulnerable – fragile might be a better word. It is clearly possible to put in months of work and *not* get an order at the end of it. This is expensive, and it colours much about the sales activity in an organisation where this is the case, not least making who is pursued very important, but making the quality of communication vital at every stage.

Size of business

The size of a 'piece of business' is usually large. If the bottle manufacturer gets an order for the shampoo bottles then it may be worth a great deal of money and it is likely to repeat (ie, the toiletries company orders so many per month, a situation that might continue for some years). Alternatively it may be that a single one-off order is large and therefore worth an elaborate process leading up to it to achieve success (as with a construction company building one office block).

Personal involvement

Another characteristic, one applying especially to services, is when the people selling are also involved in the delivery of the service. This is true of the advertising agency mentioned above; also of accountants, architects and bankers. Here customers want to deal not with a sales 'front man', but with someone who they know will be involved in the work done; so the creative director of an advertising agency must, in part, be a sales person.

Number of customers

The kind of complexity being discussed most usually applies when there are smaller rather than larger numbers of customers. For example the potential customer list for the bottle manufacturer is much smaller in number than for a company selling something bought by every office in the land.

Size of customer

This links to both size of business and number of customers. A company with many customers, but with a small number that are disproportionately important because of their size, will tend to have business development roles with their largest customers. A company selling chocolate, say, has a completely different job to do in selling to the major chains of supermarket and to the corner newsagent.

Repeat business

The complexities tend to be greater when the business opportunity is to sell on a regular, or contractual, basis rather than seeking a one-off order.

These kinds of factors can be picked and mixed as it were. Not all may fit a particular case, but a number of them will, and when that is so, then business development tends to be the order of the day.

Product examples

Given the necessarily imprecise nature of the borderline between selling and business development, it may be useful to link what has been said so far to some examples of specific industries or products. The following are selected from amongst many examples to show the breadth of the area we are talking about:

▌ *Hotels:* a hotel may sell itself to individuals, but larger corporate clients need a business development approach. Certainly the holiday hotels you see in the travel brochures have a complex job to do relating to the tour operators who put them there and communicating with them on a regular basis.
▌ *Advertising agency:* as mentioned earlier this involves a business development process, as do many business services, from a market research company to a professional service like a corporate law firm.

■ _Computer systems and software:_ you may buy a pack containing a software disc in a variety of ways. If you get it from a major chain (such as PC World) then the relationship between the producer and such an outlet will be complex. The relationship between a supplier and a major corporate account seeking to buy a networked system of some sort, and wanting tailor-made software to go with it, is even more complex.

■ _Own brands:_ a company making, say, tonic water may sell its product in a variety of ways, but if it wants to pursue the own-brand route then it has to set up a complex process with one or more chains of retailers who themselves sell in that way.

■ _Kitchens:_ kitchen fittings (and equipment) are sold to retailers and in various other ways including direct from manufacturer to householder. Another route, demanding a business devel-opment approach, is when a manufacturer approaches house developers with the intent of persuading them to put their kitchens in all the new houses the developer builds.

Top tasks
Rapid response

You work for a major charity that has a remit to bring relief to those affected by natural disasters. You wake one morning to find the news programmes full of reports of a major disaster – freak weather has caused flash floods which this time have inun-dated a major city. Thousands are dead and tens of thousands are in need of urgent help. In the office, emergency meetings decide to launch an immediate appeal. The urgency is clear: help must be provided soon or it will be useless to many.

As the origination of a publicity campaign is put in train, thoughts turn to how money can be actually collected. You need support from the banking world (everything from special accounts to collecting tins in every branch). Your task is to persuade the banks to support the initiative and to do so within days. How do you approach them and how do you make a case that they will agree to without prolonged deliberation?

Again, these examples illustrate both the breadth of different situations involved and the wide range of products with which those people in business development roles can find themselves dealing. Furthermore, the principle extends beyond such commercial areas as have been chosen as examples so far. A charity may want to encourage sponsorship. This might be in many fields; one might be the arts. In this case the business development process (whatever it might be called in such an environment) would work in a similar way to others described and be directed at concert promoters or others chosen and targeted as suitable.

Key account management

There is again an overlap here. Account management is a form of business development and business development can involve a form of account management. Certainly account management, which as has been said elsewhere goes by a number of names (major or national account management, for example), has its own discreet approaches. If this is an area that interests you then there are books focusing solely on this process.

The situation stems from a, perhaps curious, fact that we have previously touched on and which is known as the 80/20 rule, described below.

The 80/20 rule

This is the business name for what actually stems from Pareto's Law (after the Italian statistician who noticed and documented the phenomenon). In the sales context it says that, as a general rule, 20 per cent of an organisation's customers will produce 80 per cent of the revenue from the market. This ratio may well be true of other factors too, ranging from profit to the amount of sales time that needs to be directed at them.

The percentage will vary somewhat – this is not an exact science – but the overall ratio is consistent. This alone explains something of the importance of major customers and also explains the lengths gone to in order to obtain and manage their business.

With that in mind one must take on board another principle. Major customers are not just larger than other customers – they are different in nature; and they need a different approach to sell to them and manage their business. First, the largest players in a market have more power than others. In fast moving consumer goods (FMCG products) sold through supermarkets, the vast majority of sales in the UK go through five retail giants. The situation is similar in other parts of the world. Secondly, they exhibit different characteristics as organisations and therefore need different approaches in handling them: they are more demanding, have very particular expectations and a variety of people within them who have to be satisfied. Hence key account management. The sales people who handle and sell to these kinds of account have a big job however you measure it, and there is a great deal hanging on their success.

Such selling demands that many things are handled in a very different, and usually more sophisticated, way from that necessary for smaller customers. Such factors include:

▌ having high quality information about them (detailed, up-to-date and accurate);
▌ analysis and planning;
▌ strategic thinking;
▌ links and overlaps with marketing and promotion;
▌ creativity of approach.

Often sales and marketing operate together to provide a seamless campaign to maximise the business obtained from these important entities.

As just one example of the complexities and challenge involved here, the box below shows a list of factors that are all part of any negotiation between a company and a major customer. All these factors involve cost. If the customer gets everything they want, profit may disappear. If the company is too dogmatic then there may, at worst, be no order. The old saying that you don't get what you deserve, you get what you negotiate, is certainly true in sales.

Major customer power

The kinds of thing a manufacturer (taking FMCG products as an example) might be pressed on include:

- additional time from the field sales force (for instance to help merchandising);
- discounts (and there may be many different bases for them, such as quantity bought or when purchase is made; and some are retrospective);
- any special packaging and packing;
- delivery (maybe to multiple locations), labelling; credit terms (and beyond);
- returns and damage arrangements;
- advertising and promotional support;
- merchandising materials and assistance;
- training of customers' staff;
- financing (including special credit terms).

These sorts of cost are, of course, all in addition to normal production and distribution costs. Yet major players can make demands here that quickly pose a threat to margins, knowing that the pressure for the supplier to maintain a relationship with them is intense. On the other side, a buyer – say a retailer – does not want to alienate a supplier and miss the opportunity of profiting from selling a good product. So realistically a balance is necessary; it is however one that the supplier may sometimes think tends to be one-sided. Managing such a delicate relationship is a challenging job. Again, this serves to illustrate how any special sales situation characterises the job(s) of working in it.

To round off our consideration of major customers here, perhaps the following apocryphal story (quoting less seriously from my book *Everything You Need to Know about Marketing*, published by Kogan Page) makes the power of the buyers in such companies clear:

Buyers are a tough lot

It is any buyer's job to get the best possible deal for his company. That is what they are paid for, they are not actually on the salesmen's side, and will attempt to get the better of them in every way, especially on discounts.

This is well illustrated by the apocryphal story of the fairground strongman. During his act he took an orange, put it in the crook of his arm and bending his arm squeezed the juice out. He then challenged the audience, offering £10 to anyone able to squeeze out another drop.

After many had tried unsuccessfully, one apparently unlikely candidate came forward, he squeezed and squeezed and finally out came a couple more drops. The strongman was amazed, and, seeking to explain how this was possible, asked as he paid out the £10 what the man did for a living. 'I am a buyer with Ford Motor Company' he replied.

Buyers are not really like this; they are worse.

It is difficult to summarise an area like business development, which despite its particular nature, still ranges wide. Someone in business development may be a senior sales person with a particular focus. Or they may have sole responsibility for a small number of key accounts and the large volume of business that comes from them (in some fields it might literally be one customer that is managed). They may be a senior manager in an organisation without dedicated sales staff, or have a specialised function in a service organisation linked to the service provided (like the creative director of an advertising agency) who also has a clear sales role and responsibility.

Whatever the precise role – and one could list many more functions – all such jobs are a challenge. They all demand a variety of skills. They are all creative rather than mechanistic. Those employed in them are key players at the sharp end of the business world and confirm the old maxim that 'nothing happens until someone sells something'.

45

So far a number of different industries and fields of endeavour have been mentioned and with them the products and services they produce and sell. Just what the product or service being sold is makes a considerable difference to the jobs involved in selling it. It is to this aspect of the choices to be made in contemplating a sales career that we turn next.

5 Selling what?

Profit comes only from outside an organisation. It must relate to its market place, and produce and sell products or services that customers want to buy if it is to be successful. In any aspect of the marketing process, people deciding to work in it must elect to involve themselves with something – yet the profusion of products and services increases every day. There are those who say that selling is a generic skill, that if you can sell one thing successfully, then you can sell anything – well perhaps practically anything. Which reminds me that despite the cracks about 'selling refrigerators to Eskimos', this does happen – Eskimos need refrigerators not to keep their food cold, but to keep it warm enough to cook without defrosting; sorry, I digress. Certainly there are plenty of choices about what product or service to get involved with in terms of a sales career. What is more, because you are so intimately involved with the product – and with its customers – in selling, it is a choice that matters: you should choose carefully.

Whatever the truth about selling being a generic skill, and some product areas are surely specialised and need special skills, what you sell inherently characterises the job of selling it. Some fields may be good stepping-stones (we return to this) and that alone may have merit. Otherwise you need to consider how the nature of the sales job in different fields varies and to what extent each might suit you.

For the most part the consideration, and the focus, of this chapter is on the product or service involved. After all there is all the difference in the world between toothpaste and, say, ball bearings (which would crack your teeth even if you could get them to stay on the toothbrush!) There are, more seriously, big differences in the sales task they involve and what that is like as a job. But there are other factors to bear in mind, albeit linked to the nature of an organisation; some are discussed below.

Location

The location that you work in obviously affects life style. It may or may not be important to you. Some sorts of companies cluster in particular locations. For example, in the UK pharmaceutical firms seem predominantly to be in the south east of England, many financial institutions are in the City of London, most china producers are in the Potteries, retailers are in high streets and shopping centres and those catering for the agricultural market tend not to be found in cities. This is perhaps something about which you should take both a short and long-term view; a location you favour now may be different from one that suits if you have a young family to bring up. Many aspects of location are important, even for example the fact that in a central location to which people commute, there may be little social contact amongst staff who could live far apart in opposite directions.

Many field sales people, of course, work a territory. They may live central to that territory, work predominantly from home, and the organisational office to which they relate may be located elsewhere and visited only infrequently. One advantage here for some people is being able to live in the country yet work for a large organisation based in a city.

Breadth of operations

This too will affect location. A company involved in or intent on a purely regional role will usually locate in that region. Size may also affect the resources and budgets they have available (including their budget for staff) and the scope of jobs there may be limited by comparison with a larger and more broadly based concern.

International involvement

If you want to travel, or relocate abroad on either a temporary or permanent basis, then you really have to aim ultimately to work for a firm which is, in some way, involved internationally. If you speak a second language, that may be an asset, but might also limit potential travel to areas where that language is spoken. Maybe your ambitions can only be realised by learning another language.

People

Work involves you with people: colleagues, staff, and in selling, of course, with customers. Some people you like and some you do not; perhaps a few you even hate. While you do not have to like all those people you work with sufficiently to want them to come to dinner, there could be certain kinds of people with whom you would prefer not to work. One can certainly apply the same sentiment to customers. This is not intended to be censorious. It is just a fact of life that most of us get on better with some kinds of people than others. You may want to avoid being tainted by the grey of accountants. You may want to select an environment where the majority of people will be women, or men. Another aspect of this is age. Do you want to work with a group of people who are predominantly your own sort of age? All such factors are considerations, and there are choices to be made about what will and will not suit you in this regard – most especially with regard to those you will sell to, for you will spend most of your time with them.

Level of pay

Some industries pay better than others. Which are which depends on the current situation and changes over time. The information technology industries have been paying well of late, but could be eclipsed by something else. I began my career in publishing, renowned then and now for being a poor payer; I might still be in it if plans to marry had not necessitated more money. The size of organisation may also have a bearing, as may whether it is in the private or public sector.

Fit with temperament or skills

Clearly there has to be a fit here. High tech industries are not for those with no computer skills and no interest in such things; however, most sales jobs involve some computer use. Jobs that rely on the written word a lot will not attract those who cannot write three consecutive words in a logical order for a written proposal. A creative streak might attract you to an advertising agency or a firm selling fashion products.

Level of risk

This links again to your temperament. While industry, as the introduction made clear, does not offer the wholly safe career paths it used to do, some fields are inherently more risky than others. Some organisations too have particular attitudes to this: like the US firm which said it operated a policy of 'planned insecurity'. Asked to explain, it said that 'We fire whoever is bottom of the sales league every month.' Some people thrive in this sort of environment, but not, of course, all.

Culture

This is an important one. There is culture in the sense of purpose. You may prefer to work for an organisation 'doing something worthwhile', however you define that. It might mean a charity (they are big business these days), or a health care operation. There is also culture in the sense of atmosphere and the kind of people who work there. I would imagine there is all the difference in the world in working for, say, the Disney organisation and a shipbuilding company. Few, if any, organisations do not have any need of people in sales roles.

Ethical considerations

You may not want to flood the world with military equipment (or toilet cleaner either if it is going to kill every fish within a hundred miles of your customers' drains). This is an area of serious thinking for some.

There is certainly the basis for decision here. Realistically most people are conscious of their choice involving a degree of compromise. So be it. At least you need to think the issues through, and make a decision that you can live with and which is most likely to give you what you want.

Next we will examine some main divisions, putting potential employers into separate major camps with different characteristics, and linking to a degree with the different kinds of job already touched on. As we do so we can define some more of the jargon that seems to pervade the world of sales and marketing.

Consumer, industrial or business-to-business product selling?

Consumer goods

Let us be clear first what this term means. Consumers are customers in the sense of the public – you and me going to the shops. The core area of consumer products are referred to as FMCGs – Fast Moving Consumer Goods, those things that, literally, turn over fast because consumers want to make routine purchases (buying household products like soap and toothpaste regularly). I once heard the marketing director of the division of ICI that made shotgun cartridges speak at a conference. He began by saying that his product was the fastest moving in the room! Maybe stretching the sense a little.

Consumer product marketing is perhaps the high profile end of marketing. It is what many people think of when the word marketing is mentioned. It is characterised by being:

▌ very visible – these are products seen everywhere;
▌ directed at large markets – everyone is a customer for tooth-paste (well, except maybe the guy who sits next to you on the bus);
▌ promoted in many media – from television to glossy magazines;
▌ backed by large budgets, especially for promotion – which are necessary to reach the large markets and to do so repeatedly;
▌ highly competitive – in many product areas there are many companies making essentially similar products;
▌ reliant on the creation of 'brand image' – the product name (and the whole 'personality' that goes with it);
▌ creative in approach – witness the style of many consumer advertisements (though these may well be originated by the advertising agencies much used in this sector to plan and organise the promotional campaigns).

In consumer marketing many of the largest firms have a string of brand names, and all need marketing. Sometimes this is apparent, as with the many products marketed under, say, the Nestle name. Other companies use a list of different brand names and the association with the main company is not featured strongly (as with Lever Brothers).

So, life spent marketing consumer goods is certainly in the heartland of the marketing world. Opinions differ. Some people feel that this is the only *real* marketing. Certainly it is a sophisticated form, one that utilises the full panoply of marketing techniques. Others, for whom the product itself is important, feel that the product areas involved are not the most interesting. It is worth thinking this through. You may not instinctively feel that helping sell, say, washing up liquid is your life's work, but do not overlook the fact that the competitive pressures and challenge of making anything successful in the market place are just as real whatever the product.

It should also be noted that the sales jobs in this area are somewhat polarised. Some jobs, for example that of merchandising/sales, are among the less sophisticated, but others, negotiating with big supermarket chains controlling as much as a fifth of the total market, are key – as are the people who do them.

Industrial products

This phrase tends to characterise a very different area of marketing, that of 'heavy' goods sold to industry rather than to 'Joe Public'. Again there is a wide range. It includes a considerable involvement with engineering; the product might be machine tools or products necessary to them (from spare parts to specialised oil). It includes complex items such as ships or space shuttles. It also includes a mass of products necessitated by what is called 'derived demand' – as with the example quoted of a company manufacturing and selling bottles, they might be bought by a brewery and filled with beer; the success of the beer in the market dictates how many bottles are sold. But the design of the bottle may be such that it helps produce an attractive image and sell the beer. Wheels within wheels. Cheers.

Top tasks
On your feet

You are the business development manager for a large accountancy firm. The organisation has been short-listed by what would be, if you complete the process successfully, a major new corporate account. The next stage is a formal presentation to the company's board. You are one of three people who will speak at this; what is more you have been asked to set up and coordinate the whole process despite the fact that both your colleagues are senior fee-earners. Neither wholly appreciates the need for the presentation to be first class: talking about technical matters they seem to assume that they can 'wing it' with little preparation.

How do you, first, get them to join with you to prepare something really special, and secondly, how do you act to create a presentation that will differentiate you from the other short-listed firms and win you this important piece of business?

There is some variety here, but industrial product marketing is characterised by:

▌ there being an inherently smaller number of potential customers – everyone may need toothpaste, but I for one do not have or want an industrial lathe in the back bedroom;

▌ often involving long lead times as products are designed and engineered – a new car may take four or five years to produce, but a new airliner twice that time;

▌ addressing 'professional buyers' – often people paid to buy and trained to get the deal they want;

▌ people working in it perhaps needing a technical background, qualification or understanding – this will vary of course but can be extreme (the lowest form of life in some sales departments has a PhD in nuclear physics). There are plenty of opportunities in sales for those with specialist technical knowledge or qualifications;

▌ more specialist and targeted approaches – it is wasteful to advertise, say, heat exchangers on television, but advertisements in technical journals still need to do an effective job;

▌ personal selling maybe having a more important role here – the
final link in the chain is often a personal contact and nothing is
going to be bought without it.

Sales and business development is just as necessary in these areas
and for those with a technical bent the product areas involved
may be inherently more interesting. The choice is wide.

Note: industrial marketing and the next category are not
precisely separated. There is an overlap.

Business-to-business products

The term 'business-to-business', which is how industrial products
are sold, is self-apparent and came into use as a phrase more
recently than industrial marketing. The difference is primarily that
this term omits the heavy end of industrial marketing.

So products here are those bought by offices and factories,
and by what has recently become known as the SOHO market
(Small office, Home office). They include a vast range of
things. The following is a pure miscellany by way of example:
telephones (and telephone systems), office furniture, paper-
clips, computer disks, technical journals, stationery, business
books, and cupboards (on the basis that even the business that
has everything needs somewhere to keep it!) There is a further
overlap with computers, software and other high-tech product
areas mentioned later in this chapter. Essentially here are all
the products a business must buy to keep itself and its people
in business.

Brands are important here just as they are in consumer
markets, indeed some brand names appear directed at both (you
may see a Mercedes car as an attractive prestige product, and
then find a dirty delivery van outside your door with the same
logo on the bonnet). So here again the career choice is considerable and the relationship with your own attitudes and interests
important. But there is another category that, again despite an
overlap with what has been mentioned already, is important –
not all products are products.

Services

Some products are services. These may be sold to the consumer sector: like dry cleaning, tax-free savings accounts and film processing. Or to business and industry: like industrial design, contract ploughing and staff training. Or to both: like accountancy, insurance and travel. Again you will find a moment's thought shows that there are many examples.

How is the selling and marketing of services different from that of products? Services:

▌ Are intangible – the fact that they cannot be tested by potential customers in advance of purchase in the same way as a product can, certainly makes for a different approach to marketing and more so to their selling.
▌ Are inextricably bound up with service – they are the 'people businesses' and marketing and the organisation of delivery of the service overlap; sales people are literally part of the service, even more so than in other fields.
▌ Interface very directly with customers – much more closely than in some other businesses.
▌ Allow change and flexibility to be greater, and sometimes easier, than in other kinds of business (producing a new insurance policy, say, is inherently easier than producing a new jet fighter).

The immediacy of services appeals to some people more than others. It is also worth bearing in mind the way in which services have grown in importance in recent years. This is especially so in countries like the UK, which have seen their old manufacturing base decline.

Having defined things to this extent, and with some overlap continuing, we can look at two further 'sectors' affording career choice: social marketing and specialist industries.

Social marketing

This phrase describes what has become a major force in the world, and certainly one of opportunity for people intent on using their persuasive skills. Traditionally, the term 'marketing' was used to describe effort designed to produce profit. But not every organisation is profit making. Well, some fail to make a profit despite their best efforts, but here I am identifying those that do not *want* to make a profit. It should be remembered that only the tiniest amount of money makes the difference between breaking even and making a profit or loss; in other words achieving whatever financial out-turn may be required always needs some skill. Social marketing is the province of organisations in three main sectors, discussed below.

Charities

These days many charities are, by any definition, big business. Their target market is contacted to produce funds, and marketing methods may be used in different ways (to change public or government attitudes, for instance), but marketing is real and important for them and they need marketing talent to achieve their aims and fulfil their charitable purposes. Whatever titles they may use they employ people in what are clearly sales and business development roles. Such organisations are an interesting option for some of those choosing a career direction.

Government

Both local and national government have marketing operations. These may be on a grand scale, as with advertising to highlight the dangers of drinking and driving or the need to adjust to self-assessment taxation systems. Or they can be smaller and more local, as with local authority schemes to help small business. Sometimes the target of such marketing is more bizarre. In Singapore, where I work regularly, the government messages are much in evidence. At one time, when population increase was seen as being desirable, television advertising called for people to fall in love. I contemplated writing in to say my visit was only four or five days long but that I would do my best, but felt the relevant Ministry would probably not see the funny side of it. Nevertheless there are significant and interesting opportunities here for some people, though job titles with the explicit word 'sales' in them are less likely to be seen than in industry.

Quasi-government and others

The above category overlaps into a whole range of other bodies: government agencies, trade organisations (like the Wool Marketing Board), educational establishments and professional bodies (such as the Institute of Chartered Accountants, which promotes the merits of working only with an accountant with the appropriate qualifications). Again marketing is much in evidence and career opportunities in sales and business development exist for those who see this sector as interesting or worthwhile, though personal business development is usually something that involves only small numbers of people.

Specialist industries

Of course industries differ. Part of the choice in careers in the commercial world hangs around this and how individuals see themselves. Some industries are very specialised (not so much technically, but in ways that affect their marketing and the people who undertake it). The following are mentioned by way of example, but it may be worth examining others for similar sort of factors.

Hi-tech and information technology

The world of computers, of the Internet and of hi-tech products both for consumers and industry is certainly specialised. It can be high risk and change can occur radically and rapidly (how long after fax machines arrived would you have wanted to work for a company making telexes, and how long will we see fax machines continue selling now e-mail has become so well established?) Companies in this sector are often internationally based; many are foreign owned. This is the sort of challenging environment that appeals to many people.

It tends (it is difficult to be definitive about such an area) to consist of organisations that employ younger people, that are less formal than many and that expect a lot in return for the higher than average remuneration they often pay. It is a field in which you would expect to move job more often than in some others.

But it is certainly a driving force in modern industry and worth a look for many. (Another book in this series, *Getting a Top Job in IT*, may be helpful.)

Professional and business services

This phrase encompasses a clutch of businesses that sell their expertise. Principally, it consists of those who regard the word 'profession' as being spelt with a capital P and demands qualifications of their professionals. They include accountants, lawyers, surveyors and architects. It is a category that is usually broadened to include a range of consultants (from consulting engineers to executive recruiters), property firms and more. It also has a good deal in common with business services such as market research and an overlap with financial services. One might link this area to another, that of marketing services: advertising agencies, public relations and other consultants all have business development staff. A common factor here is that those selling are also involved in other aspects of the business (for example in my business area of training – it is, for the most part, the trainers who do the selling).

Pharmaceuticals

The companies that research, create, test and then market drugs and associated products to the medical world are certainly a special category. The market is dominated by a few large players; most are international companies. This field is heavily regulated (and quite right too, say I; I do not want to grow scales after taking a cough medicine). They are competitive, but also profitable – discover and patent a cure for some major nasty and the money will roll in for years. Well, I simplify – everything needs marketing and the job of selling to doctors and hospitals is a challenging one. There are also many products that require no prescription (OTC or over the counter medicines), and these are akin to FMCG products in the way they are marketed. Sales staff here are very specialised, so too is the terminology used to describe them (the term 'medical representative' is favoured over 'sales person' and the process of selling to doctors and specialist medical staff is called 'detailing').

Top tasks
Respecting time

Customers are like so many others in business – busy. You sell a good product, get on well with your customers and are adept at explaining and making a persuasive case on behalf of your organisation. But times change and increasingly customers do not have time for you. You just get a meeting going well, when they are looking at their watches and muttering about _another meeting_. You bite the bullet and ask some of them about it, and discover that you are right – they do find your approach professional and like both what you say and the product, but complain they just do not have time for it.

Calculating that currently you tend to take three-quarters of an hour to run through a full statement of your case, you set about rethinking how you do it. Can you achieve as much in half an hour? And what could you usefully do in 20 minutes?

'Selling' needs defining too in this context. The contact is with doctors who may, as a result of what they are told, decide to favour a product, but even so they cannot place an order. If or when someone comes into the surgery with the appropriate complaint, then they can write a prescription and the patient taking this to a pharmacy will result in a sales increase. Other industries too have this disassociation between sales action and the actual purchase of the product (such as selling building materials to architects). This is the area of 'missionary selling' mentioned in Chapter 3.

The pharmaceutical area is an example of an industry that is more exclusive – people are often expected to have experience of it and people move between industries less often. Although it is as commercial as many others, some people like this sort of field because it is inherently worthwhile. And, let us be honest, some products are pretty frivolous – for instance, do you know that there is a Japanese washing up liquid on the market, which is wholly dedicated to washing fruit before eating it – the fruit not the washing up liquid? Really!

Financial services

Everyone loves to hate the banks, and this sector contains much more than the traditional banking organisations. If you feel that money makes the world go round then you might consider that this is an industry to become involved with; certainly it offers services that will always be needed. Again there are many changes in train. Branches are closing, postal and telephone accounts reign supreme and Internet accounts are growing apace. A suitable element of service must remain, and customers want to have trust in financial institutions.

Such an industry spans the old and the new. Make no mistake, much about it is very traditional (and by some standards still slow-moving) but changes will doubtless continue and it will be largely the marketing people who make them happen. You could be one such. In aspects of the business, for instance insurance, selling the product demands mandatory qualifications and you need to recognise the technical nature of much that goes on here.

There is no space here to review every industry. Many have particular and sometimes topical characteristics that make them a good fit for some people. Industry is not the only differentiating feature of potential employers, however, so on to another.

Fishes and ponds

A prime difference affecting the circumstance in which different people find themselves working relates to the size of their employer. Some organisations are big, some are not. Bigger may not just mean larger, it can mean different. A large organisation may:

- pay better;
- provide internal prospects of advancement;
- have greater resources (of all sorts);
- produce a more social environment (there are probably more people: that's a start);
- look better on your CV in terms of the impressiveness or otherwise of your career record.

Also, sales jobs in larger companies may themselves be 'larger', having greater responsibility and scope. A top job in such a company may be high profile within an industry, especially if it involves a product that is a brand leader.

Or, of course, this may not be true. Large firms vary amongst themselves as do all others. There are those people whose job in a smaller organisation exhibits all, or most, of these characteristics. Some find the more manageable environment of a small organisation more amenable. There is a choice to be made: do you prefer to be a big fish in a small pond or a small fish in a bigger pond – or a big fish in a big pond?

Because of the nature of sales and business development jobs there are no rules here. People travel many routes to success; and some travel (and move from employer to employer) more than others. What suits you is not least in importance here, and it would be profoundly unsatisfying to spend long in any kind of organisation with which you just did not fit or with which you did not have sympathy, however successfully you might perform in it.

A sure route to the top

The one sure way to the top job in a company is to start (or take over, I guess) the company. I took that route, moving from being a director of a company with a hundred plus professional consultancy staff, to setting up my own enterprise. I have enjoyed both aspects of my career. My firm may be small, but it is mine!

Seriously, considering such options makes the full variety of sales careers clear. In a small firm – whether it is your own or not – all the administrative things that you take for granted in a big company suddenly come into sharp focus. Want something to go in the post? Then you walk to the postbox. But control is absolute, and being able to do what you want is very much part of some people's brief for a good work situation. For example, latterly in my old company my work in Singapore was sometimes regarded as a distraction taking me away from the main work scenario. I like that part of the world and made an effort to maintain the continuity of work there. Now, since I have been the boss, I do not think there has been a word of criticism about my trips – not even once!

And they fit well with other things to create the work pattern I want (a little of this book – as with *Getting a Top Job in Marketing* – was typed on a laptop sitting by a hotel swimming pool in Singapore).

Starting your own business is an option and is one that will definitely involve sales. It certainly jumps you to the top, though it puts a wide range of responsibilities directly and firmly on your shoulders, all of which must go well if the business is to flourish. Many small businesses, perhaps founded by someone with great competence in whatever the firm does (graphic design, say), founder through lack of skill and expertise in sales and marketing. So, if you can find the right business, then as a business developer you may have a head start. Experience may be necessary (except, if you believe the hype, in the area of e-commerce) so it may not be something to do at once. But it is an option.

An opportunity

It should be regarded as a strength of sales and business development as a career choice that it offers so many options (and there were other options reviewed in Chapter 3). I make no apologies that this chapter has not provided a clear and infallible way of making definitive choices; that is the nature of the beast. But choices do need to be made and it has been the intention to provide guidance here on the criteria you need to keep in mind as you make them.

Career structures in this area are not especially rigid. You may well be able to change, moving from say a small company to a larger one, switching industry or whatever. Indeed this can happen several times. You should always remember though that we all spend a long time at work, certainly over a lifetime. Making the choice to go into sales is important, and selecting the area of business of the organisation you work for is important too. Think carefully. It is possible to change, indeed you may pick something specifically as a stepping-stone. But at any particular moment you want to enjoy what you are doing. So aim for what you think suits you best, aim high and go for it.

6

Management's sales role

In this chapter we examine two separate issues: sales as a part of the work portfolio of senior people whose work role is also concerned with other things, and the management job that is specific to sales – those people who manage and direct teams of sales people.

Why management sells

Selling is a task that is conducted on a wide front, and it is by no means only those people with a full-time sales responsibility that do it. There are several main reasons why managers (and a variety of different kinds of managers too) are involved in selling; they are discussed below.

Lack of sales people

There are a number of kinds of organisation in which the normal form of operation excludes sales people. One such area is that of professional services firms. If a prospective client contacts an accountancy practice, a law firm, an architect's office and other firms selling their expertise, they are unlikely to be dealt with by a dedicated sales person. They will talk to a professional – an architect, a surveyor or whatever. Why is this? Primarily it is because that is what clients want. They expect to talk to – and make a judgement about – someone who is, in the event of them doing business with the firm, going to be involved in the delivery of the service. So, the professional staff must be able to sell. Moreover they must be able to competently deploy a whole range of sales skills, from prospecting to account management.

In any such business there are opportunities for those wanting to use their sales competencies to do so in the context of specialised jobs within a specific field of interest. These and other similar businesses can offer high earnings to those with the relevant qualifications. In fact all sorts of organisations may have people in top jobs one of whose prime responsibilities is unashamedly to sell; charities are another rather different example.

Senior people

In many businesses a top layer of their business is so important, and perhaps individually so large, that the processes connected with it are in the hands of senior people (the 80/20 rule referred to earlier). Sales work done here will involve sales and marketing management, but it will also involve technical people and other senior managers up to and including the Managing Director. Where businesses must be sales led, then one likely background of top management may well be sales. Because the skill itself can continue to be an asset in many other jobs, sales people can take a variety of routes to overall top jobs, provided, of course, that they have the other necessary abilities to make the switch and be successful in their new role.

Small scale

Another area in which senior people sell is in small companies (or in small divisions or sub-sections of an organisation) where the scale of the operation and its limited financial resources prohibit the use of full-time sales people. Here management sells because there is literally no one else to do so. There is a similar situation in any business start-up. Small beginnings mean that the initial group of people must handle everything, so one at least must have sales ability. This is at its most pronounced, of course, when the original start-up complement of a new business is one person! A prime reason for the failure of new businesses in their early days is that, regardless of the technical excellence of what they produce or do, the founder has inadequate ability to sell. Selling is a key resource in such circumstances and may literally make the difference between success and failure.

There is an opportunity for some people with strong sales (and perhaps marketing) skills to be involved in new businesses from the very beginning. Their involvement may be the catalyst for the business's success, and as it grows they gradually find they have a substantial organisation growing beneath them. This is another route to a top job.

Personal need

Another reason for management to have an involvement in sales is that the individual wants it. For someone in a full-time sales management job (see below) there may be a need to 'keep his or her hand in'. In other words they want a continuing involvement in hands-on selling so that their skills do not get rusty and they continue to be close to the customer interface. In addition, they may sensibly be conscious that their credibility with their sales people will be greater if they are seen to have such an involvement. Their management role is strengthened by a continuing exposure to customers and to the realities of the interface of communication between the organisation and its customers. There may also be a need for certain high level contacts to be retained by management because of the nature of the business or the demands of customers. This last links back to previous points made here.

Another area is worth a comment: that of internal sales. There are many different situations, internally and externally, in which managers cannot achieve what they want just by instructing people. There may be a need to persuade people on the same level, or higher, where there is no automatic authority. There may be cases too where, even if an instruction can be issued, it will perhaps be executed better if the people concerned really support it. In all such circumstances persuasive communication is necessary internally and those with what are effectively sales skills will do it best. To say that any management job has need of persuasive communications skills does not open up any very specific career paths, but it does reinforce the fact that these are important skills and that they have wide ranging uses.

Sales management

However expert and effective professional sales people may be, they need some support. More than that they need management and direction if they are to maximise their effectiveness as part of the marketing mix. It is not enough for a company simply to push sales people out into the field and say: 'Sell'. Usually those who manage the team are very much part of the overall management and marketing team. In a small company such people may have many tasks and responsibilities that are really general management functions.

Top tasks
All change

As a manager in an agricultural chemical company you organise and direct the sales people and activities towards distributors who in turn deal with farmers, and in various parts of the country towards the farmers, or at least the larger ones, themselves. Now the board has decided that certain products, for example weed killers, are to be repackaged and sold to domestic consumers for garden use.

The garden centres and other outlets that these revised and repackaged products must be sold to are very different to those you and your team have dealt with in the past. With the launch agreed by the board, how do you find out what approach is necessary and reorganise and extend the sales team to address the new customers in the right way?

The full-time task may be labelled Sales Manager. It may be at board level – Sales Director. And in companies with numerous sales people and extensive operations there may be both of these and a team of others controlling groups of sales people around the company's geographic area of operation. These latter may be called Area Managers or Regional Managers; a variety of such titles are used. These are the top management jobs of the sales area.

The person managing the sales team will usually handle a certain number of customers, usually larger ones, personally. There is nothing wrong with this, indeed such involvement is useful, but it can dilute the time available for the classic sales management functions and this, in turn, can leave sales less effective. Certainly it would be my observation that in industries that put suitable time into managing a sales team the investment it represents is regarded as both necessary and worthwhile. Effectively the job continues to involve those who do it in selling, and also adds a whole range of other responsibilities and broadens the strategic role on which they must focus. It is a key role, one that has a very direct influence on results.

So what tasks make up the people management aspects of these sales management jobs? Most usually the classic tasks of sales management are regarded as falling into six areas, discussed below.

1. Plan

Time needs to be spent planning the scope and extent of the sales operation, its budget and what it will aim to achieve. Achievement is organised first around targets, and setting targets, not just for the amount to be sold but also for profitability, product mix, etc, is a key task. If the product range is large it is especially important that the team's activities are directed with the right focus.

2. Organise

How many sales people are required needs calculating (not just a matter of what can be afforded, but of customer service and coverage, though the two go together), as does how and where they are deployed. This must also address the question of the various market sectors involved, looking at not just who calls on customers in, say, Hertfordshire, but how major accounts are dealt with and the strategy for any non-traditional outlets that may well need separate consideration. Organisations that sell to groups of customers that differ radically from each other may separate the different sales tasks, and even have separate sales teams.

3. Staff

This is vital. It is no good, as they say, 'paying peanuts and employing monkeys'. If the sales resource is going to be effective then it must be recognised that recruitment and selection needs a professional approach and the best possible team must be appointed. The job is to represent the firm, to differentiate from competition and sell effectively – certainly and continuously. Recruitment may be a chore, but selecting the best of a poor bunch (rather than re-advertising and starting the whole thing over again) should simply not be an option.

It is also evident from even a cursory scan of typical job advertisements how much emphasis is put on specific past experience in many industries – 'must have worked in publishing'. As people tend to be sought at a youngish stage (when they are cheaper?) maybe there is a contradiction here. Some managers might usefully contemplate more fresh blood amongst recruits. The experience route is fine, but one effect can be to encourage the duds to circulate around a particular industry, and if someone only did an average job for one company, what makes it likely that they will suddenly do better for another?

4. Train

Perhaps 'develop' is a better word to use here, as the process is ongoing. Because there is no one 'right' way to sell, what is necessary is to deploy the appropriate approach literally day by day, meeting by meeting, customer by customer and continue to fine-tune both the approaches and the skills that generate them over the long term. If the team is to be professional in this sense, then a brief induction will not be sufficient: an ongoing continuum of field development is necessary.

It is simply not possible to run a truly effective team without spending sufficient time with individuals in the field, using accompanied calls first to observe and evaluate, and then to counsel and fine-tune performance. Without this, performance can never be maximised, indeed a whole area of activity may be left to go by default. Although results show what is being achieved, figures alone cannot, by definition, show how things are being done in the field and whether performance could benefit from fine-tuning. Only by direct involvement can sales management put themselves in a position to know what action might improve performance, and take it. Many would regard this as certainly the single most important aspect of the sales management job. The reason is entirely practical – time spent on it acts directly to increase sales. Not least the process is valuable in ensuring that sales people adopt a practical and constructive approach to what they can do day to day to refine their own techniques and improve performance. Whatever the support given by sales management, the sales people themselves are, after all, the only coach who is there all the time. This is a creative and satisfying task – and a challenging one – for anyone who wants to manage others.

5. Motivate

Like development, motivation does not just happen (this is true of so much in management): it needs time, effort and consideration. Sales people, by definition, spend a great deal of time on their own and are exposed to the attrition of the attitude that can come from customers who are not exactly 'on their side'; as a group they need considerable motivation. Like training, motivation is not simply a 'good thing': it increases sales and makes performance more certain. Again sales management must work at this area systematically. It affects overall issues such as pay and other rewards (for example, any commission scheme must act as a real incentive – not simply reward past performance – and thus must be well conceived and arranged). Motivation also affects many smaller issues.

Just saying 'well done' is an element of motivation and how many managers, whatever their role, can put a hand on their heart and swear they have found time to do even that sufficiently often in, say, the last month? There is so much involved here – communication, effective sales meetings and good organisation. For example letting a sales person act without good support material to show may well make selling more difficult and thus be demotivating. This is doubly so if those struggling to do it feel that only inefficiency somewhere in the organisation has made it necessary.

So motivation has a broad remit and involves a wider group of people than the sales manager alone.

Top tasks
Enhancing sales drive

Times are difficult. The economy has become uncertain. A competitor is pressing hard and introducing new products. Sales seem to be faltering. One member of the sales force has left and is currently still to be replaced, and certain internal changes emanating from other departments are reinforcing the view that difficult times lie ahead.

As sales manager, charged with ensuring that the sales team produce the targeted level of revenue, you need to take action to boost confidence and maximise the effectiveness of sales action in the field. Will some sort of new incentive scheme help? If so, what precisely should it be and what other action should underpin it?

6. Control

Constant monitoring is necessary if the team is to remain on track and thus hit targets. Action must be taken to anticipate and correct any shortfall and this is traditionally the role of control. It is at least as important, however, to monitor positive variances. If something is going better than planned, then it needs to be asked why – maybe there are lessons to be learnt from the answer that can help repeat the good performance or spread the effect more widely.

A key area stemming from the above is that of *sales productivity*. While the individual face-to-face encounters that form the bulk of sales work have to be effective, other elements are also important. So, the concept of sales productivity is certainly as valid as productivity is in any more traditional context. We might describe it as the sales equivalent of working smarter rather than just harder. The idea of maximising effectiveness in this area is key to the sales management task; some more about this is included in the box below.

Sales productivity

Whatever quality is brought to the execution of sales calls, sales results are influenced by more than this. The other crucial factors are:

▌ _who_ is seen (the selection of appropriate prospects/ buyers/customers);
▌ _how many_ people are seen;
▌ _how often_ they are seen (the call frequency decided upon and how it varies and is used).

If these productivity factors are well organised and are worked at on a regular basis, then the overall results are likely to be improved. Excellence here is a differentiating factor between the good and less good sales people in any industry and applies, albeit in slightly different ways, to all categories of customer, depending on the nature of the business.

Productivity comes first from sales people seeing the right people, and the right organisations, and also the right individuals within larger customers where sales people may have to see several people in different departments (as in selling, say, training to a company where purchases might be made by Personnel, Training or functional departments).

Secondly, productivity comes from sheer quantity. Provided call quality is not sacrificed, then the more potential or actual customers who are seen, the more will be sold.

Thirdly there is the question of frequency. The rule here is often stated as: call the minimum number of times that will preserve and build the business. Some accounts are called on every week, others may be seen only once a year, and many in between. Anyone, and this may affect smaller companies especially, must consider call frequency very carefully. Sometimes (remembering my own time on the road) purely personal factors influence this sort of productivity. On a wet Friday afternoon in an English February I was tempted to go for a convenient call mid-afternoon – one that was en route for home and where I was likely to get a reasonable welcome and a nice cup of tea – rather than to maximise productivity.

What is the frequency that will create some sort of continuity, how quickly do memories fade, what about the industry cycle, buying cycle, seasonality or financial year? Many factors may need to be considered in making a judgement. These things and more are all important – as are the economics involved – but customer service is always important and if frequency falls below a certain level any real continuity becomes difficult if not impossible to create.

This is an area for considered action, not an unthinking reiteration of the existing pattern. The detail here makes a difference and wise management considers it is worth some time in analysis, planning and fine-tuning to get it right. The need for productivity, and the kind of work necessary to achieve it, provides another insight into the nature of jobs of this sort and the work they entail.

All in all, sales management has a wide and vital brief. Figure 6.1 shows the various tasks as a continuum, highlighting the longer and shorter-term aspects of the job.

Finding the right people, acting to retain them and working with them so that they want and are able to deliver excellent performance is the crux of the task. The quality of sales management is often readily discernible from the state of the sales team. Excellence in sales management makes a real difference. Time spent on all aspects of sales management can have a direct influence on sales results. There are whole books on the sales management job and how to do it and for some it may be an area worth further study. There are also some specialist additional work areas: sales training (either within a company or as a consultant) is one, as are other kinds of consultancy aiming to assist sales performance. These are clearly not first jobs, but they might provide a direction in which to aim, and add further to the list of top jobs in the overall sales area.

The job of recruiting and retaining a sales team and ensuring they perform effectively is a challenging one. It has all the

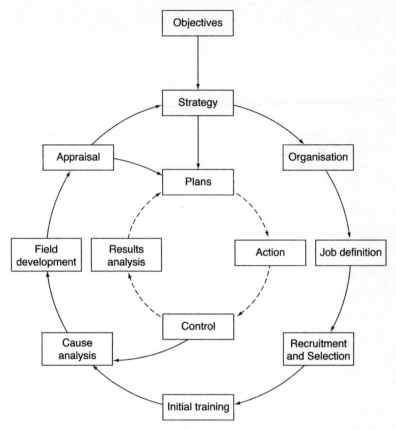

Figure 6.1   Sales management long/short term tasks and responsibilities

attributes of managing any other group of people. But managing sales people is made more challenging by the particular nature of the sales job, and by the fact that the people managed are constantly on the move and away from the office (unless, of course, we consider inside sales operations and call centres). The link with results and with the market place is in no doubt. It needs a creative approach and for some people this is the ultimate destination of a career path that begins in an individual sales job.

It should be remembered that the attributes and skills demanded of the sales person do not guarantee that they will make a good manager. The management job, as the description above makes clear, demands different skills. However, if you recognise this and have what it takes, then it is a move that can be made – and one that can extend career satisfaction.

Management titles

In considering these top jobs, it is worth noting the imprecision with which job titles are used in the sales area. There is a strong need to enhance the status of sales roles both internally and for the benefit of the individuals doing all these jobs, and externally, so that customers and others feel they are dealing with someone of suitable authority.

While sometimes 'management' titles mean exactly what they say it is as well to be aware that they may not. For instance:

▌ Core sales jobs may carry a wide range of different titles from Sales Executive to those that enhance (or misrepresent?) the job to a considerable extent: Sales Manager or Client Services Director.

▌ The area of the large, that is large customers or large portions of the business, also has a variety of jobs associated with it. Thus, partly because titles have to keep ahead of those of the core jobs, a plethora of titles are used: Key Account Manager, National Accounts Director, etc.

▌ The word 'manager' in the title is not a certain sign that the person holding it manages other people, and the word 'director' is similarly not necessarily a sign that the person concerned is on the board.

None of this matters very much in one respect. If the person concerned feels good about the job they do and how it is described, and the customers they are in touch with see it as appropriate, then maybe that is all that matters. However, in looking at job advertisements and contemplating any new opportunity, you should bear in mind the realities spelt out here. Study the title in the context of other elements, such as the salary or the kind of organisation in which the appointment will be made, and make your judgements of exactly what is being offered accordingly.

Sex

Maybe 'gender' is a better word, but I have always wanted to have the word 'sex' in the index of something I have written! Seriously, it is worth a few words to destroy the myth that 'women cannot sell'. It is true that in years gone by selling was a predominantly male province. As women became more in evidence, they were most often in areas associated with 'female products' (such as toiletries or hair preparations), or in industries where the objective of employing women was to save money as they could be paid less (publishing was, dare I say, an example of this). As more women joined the profession it was discovered that they could sell at least as well as men, and sometimes better – no great surprise there, some would no doubt say!

Now there are women in every field of selling and it is as common to find them in industrial and technical areas as in any other. Just recently, as I write, new research carried out by Dr Nikola Lane and colleagues and originally published in *The Journal of Selling and Major Account Management,* shows that teams managed by female sales managers demonstrate higher levels of effectiveness compared with those run by men. Key findings are shown in the box below; suffice to say that this is a field of endeavour in which both sexes compete equally and in which, it now appears, women may even have the edge on men. Perhaps, as a man, I may hope for more research soon!

Women in sales management

Key findings of the research mentioned above, which found an increasing number of women entering this work, included the facts that:

- Female sales managers concentrate on managing behaviour rather than just looking at sales results.
- People working for female sales managers tended to be more highly motivated and less stressed in their work.
- Better retention is achieved.

| | Female-run sales forces are more effective in a variety of ways (including levels of customer satisfaction, sales results, etc).
| | Men accept a woman manager as readily as a man.
| | But many more senior people are disbelieving of women's success in sales.

Perhaps all this should be no surprise in light of how women have become more in evidence and more successful in all sorts of business roles in recent years.

We now turn, in the next two chapters, to two particular areas of opportunity that sales work presents: those linked to international business and to e-commerce.

Top tasks
How many people?

You join an organisation as the new Sales Director. Your appointment is prompted, in part at least, by a drive for growth. New products are planned and certainly higher levels of sales are sought for the future. Currently there is a team of 23 sales staff managing territories across the country, together with a couple of National Account Managers to deal with the current major accounts. This sales resource is clearly not going to be adequate and more people will have to be recruited and added to the current complement.

The question is, how many more people are required (and will be cost-effective), what kind of people are required, and where should they be located? On what basis do you work out what action to take?

7 *International opportunities*

Those who have the necessary skills to work successfully in sales have a truly transferable career asset, geographically speaking. Potentially they can work in many parts of the world. They may do this by moving to another country or, through export sales, by regular travel to another country. How to do this and indeed whether to do this needs some thinking about, but first let us consider how it is possible. The fourth 'P' of the factors making up the classic marketing mix is place. A business may be successful on a limited geographical scale, for instance operating only in one major city. At the other end of the scale there are multinational businesses that span the globe – witness the posters you see at almost any airport in the world: names such as Sony, Coca-Cola, McDonald's, Hewlett-Packard, Compaq and many more appear everywhere. Activity that involves overseas markets, on whatever scale, can be interesting, a challenge and add a whole separate dimension to work in a variety of sales jobs.

There are further choices to be made here in terms of the elements you may want to see in your career. Essentially there are three overriding issues to consider from a personal point of view when considering whether you should aim to have an international element to your career.

Some issues to consider

1. Scale of operations

If you want to work for a large organisation, many of them are international in some way. Conversely picking an international firm usually puts you in the league of those organisations that are large. Products and services play a part here: soft drinks are needed across the globe, but some other products are more specialised and do not offer export opportunities. Such scale also relates to risk, and this is worth a thought. A large company may be stable, but it is possible to be quite a big fish in one geographic pond with a multinational, and yet wake up one morning and find that a US parent company has made some change that leaves you nowhere.

2. Travel

A personal goal may be to travel. Fine, certainly being involved with a large international operation of some sort may allow you to do just that. Travel can be something that occurs unexpectedly. In my own career, while travel was not something I sought or thought likely, company growth took an international form in part. So now I find business has taken me to most countries in continental Europe (including certain of the old Eastern bloc countries), to the Far East, Australia and New Zealand, parts of Africa and both North and South America; and to some of these on a regular basis. Most of this travel I have enjoyed; certainly once it was under way I worked at ensuring some of it continued. But make no mistake: travel can get out of hand. Living out of a suitcase, endless flights, time changes and living in hotels can quickly pall and too much time away from home can disrupt home life and career alike. This is another area about which you may want to form a considered view as you plan your future.

3. Overseas residence

To experience overseas working and avoid the disadvantages of travelling too much, some people prefer the resident route. Actually living in another country – becoming an ex-pat as they are called – guarantees a different sort of experience, though it is possible to lose touch with home base (so much so that you may come to be regarded as inappropriately qualified to work there again). Certainly this route is only for those able to adapt and fit in with the culture and way of working in another country. It may help with certain specific rungs in the career ladder; for example, a sales manager might take on the task of being resident manager in a territory and add more general management duties to his or her work portfolio in the process.

Organisational approaches to overseas markets

The world is now, we are told, a 'global village'. Certainly for many organisations success must be measured amongst world markets. The foreign currency generated by international operations is vital to the national economy, so there is also an additional worthwhile element to work that involves this. I am, on occasion, what is called an 'invisible export' (providing services) and add to these figures just a little.

An international element to your career may be something that comes, or is sought and found early on, or which develops over time. It certainly extends the definition of 'top job'. Only a very few people may become overall sales director for major multinationals, but many more may head up sales operations in a specific region or individual market doing what are certainly top jobs.

To consider career options in more detail, you need to review the range of ways in which organisations organise to explore and exploit overseas markets. Several approaches are involved and are discussed below.

Export marketing

This is essentially selling goods to overseas customers but doing so from a base in your home market. This implies physically shipping goods across the world. This may be done by the organisation itself, for example using its own fleet of trucks to ship goods to Europe or beyond. It may be dependent on the use of shippers, whether goods are to travel by road, rail, air or sea. It can be done with no support or presence in the final market; but it may necessitate some presence – indeed many people work in export sales, regularly visiting their company's customers or distributors in far flung parts of the world. This demands a high self-sufficiency and, of course, a resilience to the difficulties of regular travel and long periods away from home. It should be noted here too that the old saying, 'out of sight, out of mind' can have some truth in it; if you are cut off from much of the workings of your employer for much of the time certain aspects of active career management are made more difficult.

Export with a local presence

The form that a local presence takes clearly affects the way a company operates and thus the nature of the jobs involved. Maybe the company will have its own local office. This will link with the headquarters and may handle independently a range of things that have to be done locally (and maybe differently from the way they are done at home) – local advertising or service arrangements, for instance.

Alternatively, the company may work with an agent or distributor: in other words a local company that undertakes the local work, and marketing, on behalf of the principal. Such a company may specialise, only selling, say, construction machinery. Or it may sell a wide range of products, sometimes across the whole range of industrial and consumer products in the way that large distributors – often called trading houses – do. Sometimes such arrangements are exclusive, meaning they will not sell products for competing manufacturers; sometimes not. Payment of such entities is often on a results basis, but they cannot simply be set up and left to get on with it.

Success is often in direct proportion to the amount of liaison, support and communication that is instigated between the two parties by the principal. An active approach is necessary. For example, the distributor's sales staff must understand the product and know how to sell it. A company may well see this as an area for support: it provides training, flying trainers out to the territory and taking any other action necessary to make it work (translation of materials, perhaps). There are sales jobs here aplenty. Such entities need visiting regularly, and the likes of large distributor organisations are potential employers in their own right. Someone who knows the product and the market, having worked for their principal or another firm in the industry, may be attractive.

International marketing

This implies a greater involvement in the overseas territories, everything from setting up subsidiaries to joint ventures and, in some businesses, local manufacture. The complexities here can be considerable, with components being sourced from several different locations around the world, assembled in one or more main centres and then distributed to and sold in many markets. Such is common, for instance, in the motor market. The complexity here means that a variety of sales jobs are involved and that a sales background may be a good one for many managers to possess.

Licensing

This is an example of one of the other approaches possible. Here nothing is done on an ongoing basis by the principal. It sells the right – the licence – to produce the product to someone else. The deal may include help with a variety of set-up processes (from the provision of drawings to machinery), but thereafter the local company runs its own show and marketing, and payment is on some sort of 'per product produced' basis. There is less staff involvement here, but someone has to sell and set up the original licensing arrangement.

E-commerce

A more recent development is the phenomenon of business that may, in a sense, operate anywhere in and from anywhere in the world. This is another area of growing opportunity for sales people, though it remains specialised and volatile; there is more on this in the next chapter.

There are other methods also: for instance franchising from the likes of McDonald's, but used with a wide range of products and services. But whatever the overall marketing strategy there is a sales dimension. Products must be right, and many need adaptation for overseas markets (as with car safety features or something as basic as the melting point of chocolate sold in hot countries). Cultures and local conditions are different and the organisation and the individual people must understand and adapt to operating in an environment away from their home base. This is not the place to digress into the details of international marketing, but tackling international markets, on whatever scale, is an area that illustrates the dynamic nature of the overall sales and marketing process. The world itself is changing as we watch, new markets are opening up and, at the same time, some markets may contract, for reasons as varied as government change or natural disaster.

It is also an area where those who are involved in a sales role, or indeed in others, may not have the same level of support overseas as may be available at home. The UK sales manager may inhabit a large office, surrounded by staff and support services. The sales manager in another country may be one of a handful of people. For example, briefing a major customer may mean a visit 'up country' in a four-wheel drive vehicle on roads made treacherous by the rainy season.

In addition, always remember that there are jobs here that involve a whole additional dimension to home-based posts: that of getting to grips with a different culture. It may be subtly or radically different. Extremes may involve a sales meeting at which people must politely eat sheep's eyes in the Middle East, or trying to remember the etiquette involved in a meeting to negotiate terms in Japan. The comments of Myles Proudfoot, recently posted by Procter & Gamble from its UK office to its headquarters in Cincinnati, are interesting and perhaps have some lessons for others thinking about similar changes of one sort or another:

> So far, coming to the US has had a big impact on my career, projecting me more into the limelight than ever before. The biggest difference in my work environment has been how much closer I am to the centre of power. Being an ex-pat makes you more visible to an organisation as well as raising expectations about your performance.
>
> Being a Brit in the US is generally good news. There's the big novelty factor of the British accent. And having a name like mine really gets them going. Americans do business differently than Brits. For a start I was surprised how little humour

is used in meetings. I learned quickly to drop any attempts at irony; Americans take themselves very seriously. American humour extends to 'Would you like to borrow my video of the Patriot?' Presentation is important here and the Americans have a much more polished style than the Brits.

Working here has been different from my previous experiences, as I have moved to the corporate headquarters. I've adapted from a 'make do' mentality to an abundance of resources, people and processes that need to be followed. Why do it yourself when three others will do it for you!

How might such a move assist me long term?

I make a point of actively contacting the movers and shakers in the company, to learn from them and share my ideas. The network of contacts I have developed and wide exposure to new people are helping me to connect with the latest ideas and opportunities. This is improving my chances for exciting assignments in the future and enhancing the projects I get offered now. This type of move automatically launches you into an accelerated track of experience. At least I made sure it would before I accepted the assignment. There's also a certain kudos associated with having had a successful foreign assignment, which can open new doors of opportunity. Insider knowledge of how the US parent company works will give an advantage over the less initiated elsewhere. As I master the inner workings of the organisation, I'm beginning to understand company methods or decisions I once questioned before I came to the US.

Lastly, coming to the US has changed the way I see the business world, exposed me to new horizons and raised my expectations of what I want to do in the future.

Going back to my old job in the UK is no longer in my 'game plan'.

Beyond the differences in cultures, you might also like to consider hostile conditions. Some countries are not an automatic choice for comfort: a range of things such as climate, politics, law and order (or the lack of it) or simply inaccessibility may make them unattractive as places either to visit or to live. For some this is something to avoid, for others making a specialisation of being able to operate despite such difficulties creates a career opportunity. Recently the terrible terrorist atrocities in the USA have shown just how volatile the state of the world remains. Some career options on the international front may be desirable at one moment and virtually ruled out the next.

However you look at things it remains in most ways a big world we live in. Geography is certainly a potential decision area for many people thinking about how to develop their careers, and it is one that presents a wide choice.

8 Selling and e-commerce

Few if any people can be unaware of the change wrought on the organisational world by the information technology (IT) revolution. Whether it is just the advent of some new gizmo or a wholly different way of doing things the effects stretch far and wide. For example, we take being able to purchase a book with one click of our computer mouse for granted (indeed that may be how you came to be reading this). In fact it is a very recent development and one of the basic givens about this whole area must be an acceptance of the enormous rate of change. Hence the saying about this sort of technology and system – if it works well, then it's obsolete.

Marketing has certainly been affected by these changes, in a number of different ways, and this affects sales people both directly and in terms of the environment in which they work.

Complications

Taking certain negative factors first, consider the customer. They are as affected by the march of technology as you are, and what technology does for them may actively make life more difficult for you. Two examples illustrate.

First, customer ordering systems in many businesses are now often automated. At a supermarket checkout the till rings up the money for the customer but it also records the resulting stock level. At a particular point the computer initiates a new order to the supplier and further supplies are delivered. Much of the process in between may be automatic. Then, later, a sales person is on the supermarket's doorstep asking to see the buyer. What's the reaction? Someone might say, 'Our computer buys your product' and a meeting is declined. The sales person has a list of things he or she wants to discuss: product positioning, new promotion, display and merchandising opportunities – all these could be delayed or go by the board. It makes the job of selling that much more difficult and specific steps have to be taken to make the wanted meeting seem attractive – unmissable – to the buyer.

Secondly, products are getting more and more sophisticated. Sounds good, but this probably actually means more complex. This in turn means more product information for sales people to take on board and then put over to customers, clearly and quickly (customers will not make more time for people because they are slow, or circuitous, in explanation). This has clear implications for briefing and training – more information, more regular changes and updates. But it is an opportunity nevertheless: if sales people take all this in their stride the impression they make on people is enhanced. It is doubly useful to make sure they excel at anything competitors find difficult.

Top tasks
A different start

There is an old story of a salesman who persisted and persisted in contacting one particular prospect. Finally he is granted a meeting and, on meeting the buyer, he is told brusquely, 'Now, tell me what you want and remember, I must have had 10 sales people like you on the telephone this week asking for appointments.' Quick as a flash he replies, 'I think they were all me!' It makes a point: buyers may well see many people and what is more they may find that they not only all offer something similar, they go about things in a very similar way.

In a business of this nature, how do you approach things so that you are thought of as different (yet so that your approach will be seen as acceptable and appropriate)?

Overall, in some industries e-commerce is taking over from, or being added to, other forms of distribution. So far the things sold most successfully over the Internet are limited and fall into comparatively few categories. These include:

▌ price-driven purchases (often where the product is checked out elsewhere and only bought over the Internet);
▌ enthusiast products (eg, computer games);
▌ convenience goods (eg, buying a book that then lands on the doormat);
▌ niche products of various kinds.

The range may well widen. Meantime management must ensure that where personal selling remains possible, acceptable – even wanted – it is well deployed. It is perfectly possible to persuade some customers that it is better (for them) to buy following personal, individual advice than just by scanning a computer screen. Sales people need to be aware of the environment in which they operate, and the fact that the 'buying experience' that people participate in now includes a greater variety of processes than ever before. E-retailers are themselves, of course, a new category of customer and need selling to like any other.

Although there are dangers in many of the factors mentioned, the primary impact is positive and the moral is the same in all cases – get these things right and an organisation adds to any edge between it and its competitors.

Opportunities

There are many ways in which technology interacts with sales. For the manager the job is to see the possibilities, and to take a broad view of them. This is a new area of work and responsibility now added to a number of management jobs in sales. Some of the questions that must be asked of a possible new initiative are as follows:

▌ What will it cost?
▌ What effect will it have on productivity?
▌ How will it affect peoples' sales power?
▌ Will it have a positive or negative impact on customer service and perceptions?
▌ Will it assist in building relationships and business?

These different factors need balancing carefully. Something may seem to cost too much, but there may be dangers in ruling it out and missing significant benefits. Two improvement areas must be assessed: productivity and sales effectiveness. About the first, Stanley Roach, Chief Economist of Morgan Stanley, said: 'The productivity gains of the information age are just a myth. There is not a shred of evidence to show that people are putting out more because of investments in technology.' Harsh words, and in the sales area not borne out – but careful checks are needed to make sure that a positive effect will accrue from any technological changes contemplated. Assisting productivity may make something immediately desirable, but how will customers see it and what will it do to their perception of your customer service? It is this aspect that influences sales effectiveness most.

The following examples, in no particular order of importance, illustrate the range of areas to consider here and hint at further changes to come.

Mobile telephones

A simple one first. These are already ubiquitous and their use can certainly boost customer service and speed things up, though they should never ring and interrupt a customer meeting. They seem headed to duplicate some of what computers do, though how well they will do so remains to be seen.

Mobile computers

These, in the form of everything from high capacity laptops to simpler handheld devices (eg, Palm or Psion machines), can go into the customer meeting with the sales person. They allow a variety of things to be done quickly and easily:

▌ checking stock and placing an order for a customer from his or her own office during the visit;
▌ updating records or issuing instructions to the sales office (perhaps from the car after a meeting);
▌ forming part of a presentation to a customer (using PowerPoint charts to explain complex figures perhaps).

The net impact here should be good: saving time, adding immediacy and allowing informed decisions to be made on the spot. Clearly those in selling need computer skills at least up to this sort of thing.

Top tasks
Think of a number

Your role involves high-level negotiation with professional buyers. In the supply of construction equipment this process juggles with specification, delivery, after-sales service, spare parts and, of course, a raft of financial matters from price, discounts, buy-back arrangements, depreciation, resale values and leasing arrangements. You know the details involved thoroughly, but the actual number crunching necessary – if we changed the spec to option three, added an extra machine and paid up front that would be worth a further 1 per cent off the price, surely — is always a challenge. The buyers always seem to have figures worked out ahead of you and you are worried about looking less than professional or, worse, being rushed into a poor deal.

How can you handle the conversations with buyers in a way that allows you to slow the pace where necessary so that you can field a considered response, one where you are sure of the numbers?

Assisted learning

A variety of skills can be put over by learning packages (eg, programmed learning devices on CD ROM). This may be useful for product knowledge or sales skills, and represent another aspect of technology that a sales job may involve you with and with which you must be comfortable.

Communications

Methods have changed (when did you last get a telex or even a fax?) and e-mail has replaced many more complex messages. It takes time to get something written, printed out and posted, so the convenience is obvious. But it is not right for everything. An e-mail may fail to impress a customer because it is so informal, or so brief it fails to be clear. And it can be wiped out at the touch of a button (so may not produce any potentially lasting memory jogger with a customer), and it does not impress graphically in the way a company letterhead should. Horses for courses – a variety of methods must still be used, and this is something else for sales people to think about: always going for the easy option may dilute the overall and cumulative impression they should be helping to build.

Research and information

Information is power, it is said. Going to a meeting under-informed and showing that no trouble has been taken to find out about a new potential customer can quickly do damage. A while ago a few minutes spent on the telephone, going through reference books or getting hold of a company's annual report was worthwhile in gaining information on customers or leads. Now the ability to access the Web site of so many organisations speeds and simplifies the whole process – though more than just this may be necessary, and sales people do have to actually note information obtained and think about how it can help them sell. Some rules and guidance from management here may be valuable. Web sites are similarly a good way to gather competitive intelligence.

So, sales people should be better informed in doing their jobs than ever before; getting into that position is another important part of their jobs.

CRM (Customer Relationship Management) systems

Here there is considerable sophistication with many different software systems available to record, monitor and prompt action with major customers. The data available here are invaluable, but the mistake should not be made of thinking that the system will do it all. Contact is personal and whatever prompt is given to the individual sales person, he or she must interpret it sensibly and take appropriate action. Like many areas of systems a specific element of danger here is a lack of flexibility, with the system being followed slavishly and action directed at individual customers not being sufficiently well tailored. This is becoming quite a major area for some sales people, and there are certainly jobs that cannot be done without the ability to handle this sort of technology.

Presentations

In some industries the sales process involves the regular use of formal presentations (another important personal skill), and in these and in many meetings visual aids are often very professional looking; anything _ad hoc_ can look slapdash. Such aids are important in assisting and augmenting customers' imagination; however, they must support what is said and not take over the process. If well used they bring an important additional dimension to the sales process; if not they can lull the sales person into ceasing to think sufficiently clearly, going through the presentation on automatic pilot led by the charts or whatever he or she is using.

Web sites

Sales people have always had to link precisely with other media: they must build on the image of the organisation and take the customer further in terms of both information and image. The many organisations that have Web sites now have an additional element to assist in the process of informing customers. This may mean that by the time they talk to a sales person, customers are much better informed than in the past (and this includes the information they have about the competition, their prices, etc). A good Web site can thus make the job easier for sales people, but even small deficiencies can cause problems (if it is difficult to navigate or manifestly not kept up to date, for instance).

There are also specific ways that customer visits to Web sites can be used to enhance the sales process. First, there is research. Information can be gathered by prompting customers or enquirers to complete information (without making it mandatory or too onerous to do). A well-designed Web site can thus provide ongoing, up-to-date information about customers – their feelings, requirements and more.

Second, there is the telephone link. Software (or support) is available now to link customer visits to direct contact. A customer visiting a Web site and wanting to take things further can click on a box and prompt telephone contact. Systems can ensure this happens promptly – or even guarantee that it happens so quickly that a call is received while the customer is online: they can look at information on screen while talking to a sales person.

The possibilities inherent in this interface are broad and varied. Any technology used alongside sales contact must be well thought out. It must be customer-oriented and enhance customer service and satisfaction rather than just improving the basis for selling and the likelihood of success (though it should do this too!) There are other implications here. These include: selling overseas (where immediacy and quality of contact can be improved), and demonstration of commitment (a customer may be impressed by the contact provided by a Web site in the same way as they may see advertising support making their job of selling on a product easier). Further technological developments will extend such possibilities. Already smart cards are allowing information to be collected about customers and linked to future contact and promotion and sales. For example, customers' purchase of a particular product (paid for on a card) can be followed by sending them linked promotional material – a sales pitch to the shop where this happens may include reference to this kind of process.

We are, as customers, probably all exposed to selling practice that reflects these changes. Keep your eyes open and see what you can spot, what you think about it and whether it adds or subtracts from the appeal of the sales area. The box that follows shows the cross-over possible between personal and technological selling, with two simple examples, good and bad, from my own observation.

How selling is affected by technology

Good. Recently I contacted Oberoi Hotels in India. It was easy to search for their Web site and easy too to put a question to them through it. An hour later I had a call from their representative in London. They had a fresh, warm lead to follow up, but from my perspective as a customer they already knew something about me and tailored their approach well to the circumstances, making it seem like excellent service. This kind of thing now represents the simplest kind of technological enhancement, yet the effect on the customer is good and the chances of prompting business enhanced. In such circumstances if the next stage for the supplier is going to visit someone, then that meeting should be just a little easier to handle and make persuasive.

Bad. Recently I was visited by a financial services salesman (whose organisation better remain nameless). He arrived on time and seemed very professional, yet proved so highly dependent on technology that I rather lost patience with him. He disrupted my desk with his equipment – a laptop – and took me through a seemingly endless PowerPoint presentation the bulk of which was clearly standard, when the whole purpose of the meeting was to link individually to my circumstances. The effect was the reverse of what was intended. While the charts shown looked good, their message was distanced from the customer, and the proportion of the total message that came straight off screen diluted the impression that the salesman made in a business where personalities and their expertise are crucial. Moral: in selling, technology must always support the personal presence.

In both these cases the implications for sales management are clear. In the first, things seem to have been well organised with the customer in mind. The system worked and the individual sales person encountered had clearly been briefed as to how to work so that the separate effects on customers of what they did, and what the system did, enhanced one another.

In the second, technology seemed to have taken over. The salesman proceeded on automatic pilot, as it were, and the net effect made a sale less likely than it might have been. This was not because the technology could not have been organised to enhance matters: it could. Rather, insufficient thought had gone into deciding how the integration would be made; surely a sales management responsibility.

The modern sales manager now has the bigger job of organising not just people, what they do and how they do it, but also the considerable technology used in whatever way to back them up. The whole needs to work well together, and no element of it can be left 'just to happen', or the customers end up with an experience that works less well for them.

Conclusions

These trends are set on a course. The full implications are, perhaps by definition, unclear. In the book, *The Information Age*, Manuel Castells writes:

> The twenty-first century will not be a dark age. Neither will it deliver to most people the bounties promised by the most extraordinary technological revolution in history. Rather, it may well be characterised by informed bewilderment.

Fair comment. Technology may still perhaps be in its infancy. But already all managers must be careful to take the right view of it – and to take the right action on matters it affects. In considering sales and marketing, the three key rules should be to:

1. Take the broad view: information technology does not affect just one easily defined and self-contained area, it potentially affects everything.
2. Seek opportunities: but remember, changing technology does not automatically mean 'new = good'. Changes may present difficulties too and it is as well to be on your guard for them.
3. Give priority to customer focus: just because something is technically possible does not mean it will create positive advantage; ultimately it is the effect on customers and on customer service that matter most. Checking things out is as important as moving ahead fast.

The businesses that operate within technological areas, or which produce or sell technologically based or influenced products, will all need sales and marketing people who are up to a considerable, and very particular, challenge. Here in a short chapter only the flavour of how these changes are affecting those who work in this area can be given. It is clear that there are more changes to come. If you work in sales and marketing then you will be part of them.

9 Key attributes – skills and qualifications

In this chapter we address the matter of skills, the need for them and how to acquire them, along with the qualifications that may usefully underpin them. We also touch on the question of what characterises persuasive communication to give a feel of the sales job in action.

Everyone is born with certain abilities. All sorts of other abilities are difficult to acquire. It takes time and effort to learn to do many things – juggle with flaming torches without burning holes in the carpet, perhaps. But sales is something of an oddball in this respect. First, it demands a range of skills – in communication and personal organisation, for example – and these in turn demand both study and experience to acquire. Despite the old description of someone being a 'born salesman', there are few who, in reality, can be so described. Success, almost exclusively, comes to those who work at it, though of course some people find it easier than others. Secondly, the mix of necessary skills varies depending on the area of work – a range, as we have seen, running from managing a single territory to heading up the sales effort for an organisation with no dedicated sales resource, and more. Further, someone may have a whole package of skills, qualifications and experience and may still be precluded from certain jobs because one element – essential to that job – is missing, or because they do not have the business acumen, creativity or persistence that sales demands.

No one has 20/20 foresight, but it is worth thinking through as far as possible what skills your own long-term desired future demands that you acquire. Clearly certain specialised areas may make special demands; for instance there are marketing jobs that need:

▌ fluency in a foreign language (mentioned in Chapter 7);
▌ technical qualifications (eg, in engineering or accountancy);
▌ high levels of one particular skill (eg, negotiation for someone in an area of sales where this is part of the process);
▌ skills linked to a specific industry or area of work (eg, numeracy in financial services);
▌ a certain level of formal qualification in order to have credibility in a particular field.

Beyond that we can focus on certain common skills, and some – referred to as 'career skills' earlier because they are so often instrumental in assisting career development – that are always likely to be helpful. Many of the latter are simply prerequisites of success; they are not options.

The right skills in the right form

Skills are required in a specific form. For example, if their use is crucial to achieving sales results, then they must be deployed not just skilfully but in the precise way that the nature of the operation demands. For example, a field salesperson may not have to just conduct a customer meeting, but to do so in a very short time (eg, medical representatives calling on doctors are often fitted in amongst appointments with patients and are granted an average audience of four minutes). A key accounts manager may not just need to make a good presentation, but one that is exactly 20 minutes in duration to meet the allocation of time the customer demanded.

In other words, skills are no use if they can only be deployed in some 'perfect' circumstance: they have to be made to fit and work in the real-world situations of the organisation, its customers and its overall market environment. Whatever is being done and whatever skills need to be deployed in doing it, other factors can usefully enhance it: native wit, flexibility, a pragmatic approach, an ability to be 'quick on your feet', and more besides.

Top tasks
Which you?

Selling is not a question of acting and nothing you do must come over as false. That said your manner is an important part of what enables people to make a judgement about you, what you represent and sell. So you do need to tailor your approach to each and every customer so that they can all say, 'That's the kind of person I trust/want to do business with.'

To specifics: imagine you are young, new to the job and female. One of the first and most important customers you will deal with is a senior man, very experienced in the industry and who, in the words of your sales manager, 'does not suffer fools gladly. Don't,' he said, 'let him think you are a soft touch, someone he can run rings round and who will renegotiate their discount level.'

You are planning for your first meeting with him. The shape and structure of the meeting apart (and you must think that through as well), how are you going to come over as confident and with sufficient clout to do business with this person? What sort of manner do you adopt and what characteristics should you project and perhaps exaggerate with this person, who knows his stuff and will expect you to be an expert?

Skills are referred to throughout the book and readers should be under no misapprehension regarding the range involved and their inherent importance. In part sales jobs are a matter of flair, but much of it involves solid, considered, effective and systematic application of the skills and approaches needed to achieve success.

Qualifications

It should be recognised at once that some people in sales have little or no formal qualifications, indeed it may be that some are there precisely because it remains possible to get in, and to succeed, without some high powered degree. There are other jobs in sales where a degree, perhaps in some technical discipline, is essential. And the picture is changing. The large sales forces of old have got smaller in recent years. Fewer, but better qualified and trained people tend to be employed and for anyone wanting to get into the area, and planning to get to the top, qualifications of various sorts are becoming more and more important.

Let us review the nature of qualifications in general first. Any qualification, at whatever level, is of dual importance to anyone with an eye on career success. They are a method of acquiring knowledge and developing skills, and evidence of a level of competence in a particular area.

With a high proportion of people entering business having some sort of qualification, it is important for careerists to consider carefully what they need to do in the context of a sales career. Again some of the issues have been mentioned and there are choices to be made:

▌ Do you want to work to secure a qualification? If so:
▌ At what stage of your career do you do so?
▌ In what way do you undertake it? (Methods range from a full-time university degree course to a correspondence course or distance learning, perhaps utilising the Internet.)
▌ What area do you select? A specifically sales-oriented topic? Something broader – as broad as marketing perhaps? Or a technical qualification, one that links to the product sold or the industry in which you work?

There are both broad and specific ways of approaching these questions, and the range of options is very wide. A careful and thorough trawl through providers must be undertaken, and the relative merits of the various options assessed. It can be a daunting task. What is more it has various dimensions. You need to decide which course will be the best, and most relevant, learning experience. You must consider which will be judged most attractive by your current or other potential employers (if you know at this stage what kind of people and organisations these are likely to be). You must consider too a host of other factors, such as the social element of the experience and the location in which it will take place, especially for any full-time course.

What qualification?

This is an area for careful consideration (and therefore some advice is useful). There is no easy option here. I cannot say, 'Take this degree course and your sales career is set for success.' There are a host of options and people go into sales and succeed with everything from an HND in some specialised topic (engineering, say) to an MBA in marketing from a world-renowned institution.

Importantly, in an era of lifelong learning, people seek and obtain training throughout their careers either through interest or necessity. Such activity may span everything from attending a short course to acquiring a new qualification to add to their credentials. The question of qualifications should not be regarded as a one-off decision taken right at the start of your working life.

It is beyond the scope of this book to review every option, much less to try to place them in rank order or match the best option to particular career paths. Whatever stage you are at, if you know – or have a good idea – what you want to do, then you can relate decisions to that goal. This applies literally from subject choices in school onwards; and, of course, you need to bear in mind that early exam qualifications may open or close options at higher levels if they are required entrance requirements.

Although they are not the only providers of sales and marketing qualifications, the Chartered Institute of Marketing and the associated Institute of Professional Sales should be a prime point of reference for many people. They offer:

- a range of specific qualifications at the various levels;
- links with a wide variety of educational institutions that teach for their qualifications;
- the possibility of using different learning mechanisms (for example, they have recently linked with the Open University to make available a new Master's Degree in Marketing);
- dynamic updates to their programme (for example, the e-Marketing Award, to link with the important developments in IT and e-commerce).

A summary of their offerings in marketing is shown in Figure 9.1. It provides an overview of the different programmes and levels and the relationship between them.

Figure 9.1 Chartered Institute of Marketing qualification programmes

They offer a parallel range of qualifications through their sister organisation, The Institute of Professional Sales. Figures 9.2a and 9.2b show these qualifications in detail, and because it is arguably the prime professional body, more details of it appear in the 'Useful addresses and information' chapter towards the end of this book. Such specific sales qualifications are a comparatively recent development, and one to be welcomed.

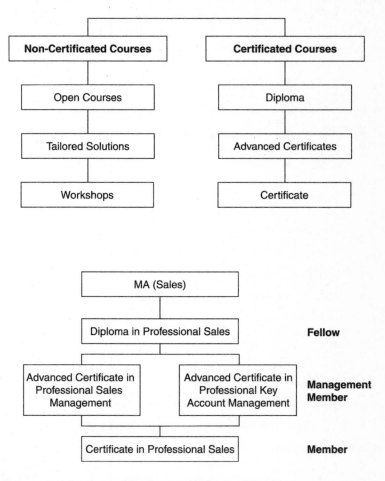

Figure 9.2a Institute of Professional Sales qualification programmes

101

Qualification	Level	Pre-qualification	Age	Delivery	Likely Current Level	Next Level
MA (Sales)		Diploma in Professional Sales		Portsmouth University	Senior Sales Manager	
Diploma	Strategic	4 years, sales experience inc. 1 at management level	28	Training Division	Area Manager or Account Manager	Senior Sales Manager
Advanced Certificates	Operational	3 years, sales experience	24	Colleges Distance Learning Training Div.	Territory Manager	Area Manager or Account Manager
Certificate	Fundamental	None	18	On-line	Trainee	Territory Manager

Figure 9.2b Institute of Professional Sales qualification programmes

A successful career in sales and perhaps, if desired, on into marketing is made more likely if you accept the premise of this chapter. That is that it is skilful work and – for all that flair can add – success is dependent on the purposeful acquisition of the knowledge, skills and qualifications that make a professional approach possible.

Good, sound and appropriate qualifications, skills and experience are the foundation of a successful career. One final point is worth mentioning here. Sales and marketing is apt to be an especially fast moving theatre of activity; indeed this may well be one of its attractions. But this can mean people are caught out. An opportunity materialises. Perhaps a project is looking for someone to take it on, but there is a specific requirement that the person chosen has a particular skill or category of experience. There is no time for someone without it to fill the gap and they may be passed over. Ditto promotion. So early decisions are important. Gradually, as experience builds, qualifications may matter less in relation to that experience, but what is learnt through achieving them stays with you throughout your career.

Of course, the ability to take on new things and learn fast 'on the run' is itself a characteristic worth having, and this alone may get some people into new areas. But one cannot rely on this. In some circumstances good luck, muddling through and winging it are not options; success comes to those with the ability to create it.

The moral is clear. Do not hesitate to fill out your range of skills, certainly those that you see a clear need for. In a busy life it is easy to leave things until the moment has passed. One minute you are saying that you have a good couple of years to get up to speed, the next you need the skill immediately and its lack puts your plans at risk. You can't anticipate everything, but you do not want to look back and regret not acting to gain an advantage. At any point in your career, and with regard to any element that contributes to it, the saddest position to be in is one for which the description starts: 'If only…'.

Ongoing growth

It has already been made clear that most – all? – career choices demand that you take a lifelong learning view of training and development. If the strengthening of your portfolio of skills is to be a continuous process, it is one where it is worth developing some good habits and practices to keep you ahead and on a path for the top. Remember too that if you are currently early in your career, then some of the things you may have to be able to do in the future may not even exist now.

The most formal version of this updating and upgrading process is that specified by the professional institutes. Although participation in the formal schemes can only occur after you are at a level where you qualify for membership (necessitating successfully acquiring the appropriate qualifications), it is worth looking ahead and understanding the process involved here.

Continuing Professional Development

The Chartered Institute of Marketing is the most relevant example here. It takes the need to keep, update and extend skills as a given. It believes that the process of so doing should be a formal one, and bestows the status 'Chartered Marketer' on those who register and satisfactorily undertake appropriate activities to ensure this development. It describes the Continuing Professional Development (CPD) process as 'the systematic maintenance, improvement and broadening of knowledge and skills necessary for the execution of professional, managerial and technical duties throughout a Member's career' and list the benefits thus; you:

- enhance your CV and improve your career development;
- keep up to date with change as it happens;
- join an elite group of professionals;
- improve your competence, job satisfaction and your prospects.

The process is described thus:

Complete at least 35 hours of Continuing Professional Development (CPD) each year for two consecutive years. Thereafter to keep your position you have to maintain 35 hours CPD each year. You should also be a full Member of CIM (either a MCIM or FCIM), and in full-time employment. If you were elected to membership after 1 October 1998, you must also hold the CIM Postgraduate Diploma in Marketing.

Your Record Card contains details of the criteria which can be used to contribute to your 35 hours of CPD. Document your progress systematically on your Card – and don't forget to collect the required supporting evidence if you intend to apply for Chartered Marketer status. If you are working towards becoming a Chartered Marketer you will need to complete the Record Card to the correct timetable.

Details of the system are available from the Institute. Here it may be worth just adding a note of the 10 categories of activity that are recognised and which help clock up the relevant number of hours (note that the relative contribution of each varies, and that clearly activity within a category needs to relate to marketing). The categories are:

1. post-qualification studies;
2. short courses;
3. distance learning;
4. language training;
5. in-company management development;
6. imparting knowledge;
7. conferences and exhibitions;
8. committee work;
9. private study;
10. meetings.

Each of these is defined in some detail, for example 'imparting knowledge' includes writing books, articles, conference papers and part-time teaching (so if you had written this book you could have added some hours to your Record Card!)

Even the relatively small amount of detail given here shows the seriousness with which the whole process is taken. This is only right given the nature of marketing, and – however it may be done – no one should go into marketing believing that no form of update and extension of experience and skills are necessary once they are established.

If you want to hit the high levels, and particularly if your definition of that includes a management role in sales and marketing, then this principle is worth emulating. One day you may wish to be part of the formal scheme, but early on you can adopt your own version of it, not just looking for development opportunities, but taking an active approach and working systematically towards your own chosen objectives. The principle involved here is an asset to anyone wanting to encourage career success.

What makes for sales excellence?

For many years I have included sales training amongst the port-folio of topics on which I conduct courses. In one way or another the same question comes up at some time on them all – what is the one key thing that creates sales success? It seems sales prompts an unreasonable quest for a magic formula, one simple trick that will act to persuade and do so in an easy and uncomplicated manner. If only it were that easy. Understanding the principles of sales techniques is not really intellectually taxing: in many ways it is common sense and this is certainly true of the basic premises from which it all stems. But there is a great deal to bear in mind, and the complexity is in orchestrating the total process in order to deploy it appropriately and tailoring the approach to particular customers. Certain things are key, not least in my view the simple prerequisite of working from a broad and deep understanding of the process that allows the orchestration process to be managed.

Top tasks
No, so now what?

Despite much groundwork, numbers of contacts, a well planned and presented (you are sure!) sales meeting as well as a written proposal, at the end of the meeting you get a firm 'No'. You want to prolong the meeting long enough to find out why and, that done, you want to develop a long-term strategy to have another go at getting another chance to pitch for business.

How do you go about it?

There are many views summarising this issue. Let me quote just one, from Mark H McCormack, the American sports marketing consultant and author (*McCormack on Selling* is worth a look). He said:

The qualities that I believe make a good salesman:

- Believe in your product.
- Believe in yourself.
- See a lot of people.
- Pay attention to timing.
- Listen to the customer – but realise that what the customer wants is not necessarily what he or she is telling you.
- Develop a sense of humour.
- Knock on old doors.
- Ask everybody to buy.
- Follow up after the sale with the same aggressiveness you demonstrated before the sale.
- Use common sense.

I have no illusions that I'm breaking new ground with this list. These are essential, self-evident, universal qualities that all salespeople know in their heads – if not their hearts.

Even the characteristics of the good sales person are controversial. One myth is that this is a profession of extroverts, yet selling has at least as much to do with listening as with having the gift of the gab and also demands a considerable degree of working alone. Maybe we can say little more than that success in selling demands empathy (because it is based on understanding and being seen to understand others), good communication skills and a need to persist and succeed (what one American psychologist calls 'ego-drive'). This does encapsulate matters, but thereafter success is in the details. Certainly it is plain that a wide variety of people, men and women, young and old, and of all sorts of different characters make a success of selling, evidenced by observation of participants on the courses I have led over the years.

Beyond that successful sales people are those who undertake

the sales job effectively. So let us end this chapter with an overview of the sales job and techniques it involves. Here what is said – about the core field sales role – aims to be just enough to illustrate the techniques deployed and to add to the feeling the book has intended to give of the job itself.

The sales job – the fundamentals

First, the basics. To be successful, field sales staff must be able to:

- Plan: they must see the right people, the right number of people, regularly if necessary.
- Prepare: sales contact needs thinking through. The so-called 'born sales person' is very rare, the best of the rest do – and benefit from – their homework.
- Understand the customer: use empathy, the ability to put themselves in the 'customer's shoes', to base what they do on real needs, to talk benefits.
- Project the appropriate manner: not every sales person is welcome, not everyone can position themselves as an adviser or whatever makes their approach acceptable. Being accepted needs working at.
- Run a good meeting: stay in control, direct the contact, and yet make customers think they are getting what they want.
- Listen: a much undervalued skill in selling.
- Handle objections: the pros and cons need debating. Selling is not about winning arguments or scoring points.
- Be persistent: ask for a commitment, and, if necessary ask again.
- Manage accounts: so as to hold existing business, and develop ongoing business across the range for the future.

With that much in mind let us turn to the approaches and techniques of selling. In the remainder of this section we examine how, if you are to sell something, you would need to view the process of being persuasive and how, by recognising what others are doing in the same circumstances, you can work with people to create mutual agreement.

So, recognising the difficulties of making any communication work, we go beyond them and look at what creates a message that acts to persuade, and see how your approach can relate to the way in which people make decisions to act.

Top tasks
A planned approach

Any sales meeting is sufficiently complex to need some preparation. This may mean a few minutes thought or a couple of hours thrashing out the way ahead with colleagues. However long it takes it is only sensible – the sales equivalent of the old maxim that 'One should engage the brain before operating the mouth.'

In a particular situation it may be vital. A first meeting with a potential new customer looms. The meeting follows considerable time and effort being spent on reaching agreement to meet. The customer is a leading player in the industry that forms the bulk of your market and it has always dealt exclusively with your competitors. Now, hearing that the main decision maker has moved on and a new appointment has been made, you see this as a chance to try again to get in there. After various preliminary contacts, the meeting is agreed and scheduled. You have to think about how you want it to go. What are your objectives? What do you need to say and how do you start? What needs finding out and what questions will do the job? Most important of all, what attitude does this new buyer take and what are his needs?

You know the meeting will not go exactly as you want and you understand the need to remain flexible, but what kind of plan do you draw up?

People are often suspicious of someone 'with something to sell' and selling, as was said early on, does not have a very good image. Your approach must reduce and get over this kind of feeling. How do you do this? We will now examine some of the key approaches using some simple product examples (selling more complex products needs similar approaches, but makes spelling out the essentials more complicated).

The process in view

Essentially you start by adopting the right attitude to the process. Before you can sell anything you are going to need to approach the task in the right way. Persuading someone must not be regarded as a process of 'doing something to people'. Rather it should be seen as working *with* people. After all, any communication inherently involves more than one person. People presented with a possible course of action will want to make up their own minds about it, indeed they will instinctively weigh up the case presented to them and make a considered decision.

The amount of conscious weighing up undertaken will depend on the import of the decision to be made. Ask someone in the office, 'Will you spare time for a drink at lunchtime so that we can discuss the next scheduled departmental meeting?', and they may hardly need to think about it at all. It is only a few minutes, they have to have a bite to eat anyway, and they already know about the meeting and want to be involved. Approach them about something more substantial – buying a car, say – and the weighing up process will involve more, maybe much more.

If you want to define selling, then it is perhaps best described as being a process of helping people weigh something up and make a decision about it. Literally, when you aim to persuade you are helping people decide (the prerequisite of agreeing to buy). It follows therefore that you need to understand how they actually go about this process. In simple terms, paraphrasing psychologists who have studied it, this thinking process can be described thus. People:

▌ consider the factors that make up a case;
▌ seek to categorise these as advantages or disadvantages;
▌ weigh up the complete case, allowing all the pluses and minuses;
▌ select a course of action (which may be simply agreeing or not,

or involve the choice of one action being taken rather than another) that reflects the overall picture.

Let us be clear. What is going on here is not a search for perfection. Most things we consider buying have some downsides. This may be the most useful book you ever read, but reading it does take a little time, and that could be used for something else. This time disappearing might well be seen as a downside. The weighing scales analogy is worth keeping in mind. It can act as a practical tool, helping you envisage what is going on during what is intended to be a persuasive exchange. Beyond that it helps structure the process if you also have a clear idea of the sequence of thinking going on in a buyer's mind and involved in this weighing up process.

The thinking process

One way of looking at what is going on is to think of people moving through several stages of thinking, as it were saying to themselves:

▋ I matter most. Whatever you want me to do, I expect you to worry about how I feel about it, respect me and consider my needs.
▋ What are the merits and implications of the case you make? Tell me what you suggest and why it makes sense (the pluses) and whether it has any snags (the minuses) so that I can weigh it up, bearing in mind that few, if any, propositions are perfect.
▋ How will it work? Here people want to assess the details not so much about the proposition itself but about the areas associated with it. For example, you might be wanting to sell someone something that needs training to use (like a piece of equipment). They might see that as a chore and therefore as a minus and might, if the case is finely balanced, reject it because of that.
▋ What do I do? In other words what action – exactly – is now necessary? This too forms part of the balance. If something seen in a quick flick through this book persuaded you that it might help you, you may have bought it. In doing so you recognised (and accepted) that you would have to read it and that this

111

would take a little time. The action – reading – is inherent in the proposition and, if you were not prepared to take it on, this might have changed your decision.

It is after this thinking is complete that people will feel they have sufficient evidence on which to make a decision. They have the balance in mind, and they can compare it with that of any other options (and remember, some choices are close run, with one option only just coming out ahead of others). Then people can decide, and feel they have made a sensible decision and done so on a considered basis.

Top tasks

Enhancing credibility

You know the product you sell is good (and you like to think you are good at making a persuasive case for it!), but you also know that the case lacks credibility. People will not simply take your word for it that the product is high quality and reliable, they want reassurance – they want to know that it works. You know you need to add evidence – proof – to your case to strengthen it and increase the strike rate of obtaining orders.

How do you go about it? What facts, figures, tests, testimonials or other elements can you add to what you say and how do you blend them in?

This thinking process is largely universal. It may happen very quickly and might be almost instantaneous – the snap judgement. Or it may take more time, and that could sometimes indicate days, weeks or even longer, rather than minutes or hours. But it is always in evidence. Because of this, there is always merit in setting out your case in a way than sits comfortably alongside the way in which it will be considered. Hence the definition that sees selling as helping the decision-making process.

This thinking process should not be difficult to identify with; it is what we all do as customers. Essentially all that is necessary in selling is to keep it in mind and address the individual questions in turn. Thus you need to:

▌ Start by demonstrating a focus on the other person – it helps also to aim to create some rapport and make clear how you aim to put things over (making clear, for example, how you plan to go through something).

▌ Present a balanced case – you need to stress the positive, of course, but not to pretend there are no snags, especially if manifestly there are some. So present a clear case, give it sufficient explanation and weight and recognise the balancing up that the recipient will undertake.

▌ Add in working details – mention how things will work and include ancillary details, especially those that will matter to others.

When you set out a case the structure and logic of it should sensibly follow this pattern. Otherwise the danger is that you will be trying to do one thing while the person you are communicating with is trying – perhaps struggling – to do something else. At the end of the day they will do what they want, so the best way forward is to work with them rather than against them.

Persuasion's magic formula

There is, if not quite a magic formula, certainly one core principle that can help make every message more persuasive. This is the concept of what are called 'benefits'. People do not buy products and services, and the same goes for ideas or anything else: they buy what these things do for or mean to them. I do not want a laptop computer for its own sake, but I do want to be able to write quickly and easily on the move. Features of the machine, that is its size, weight, portability, battery life, etc are not ends in themselves, they are only interesting or relevant because of how they produce benefits. Thus the low weight makes the machine portable, which means that I can stick it in my briefcase and write on an aeroplane journey and the increased productivity (or perhaps greater earnings) are the ultimate benefit.

The relationship here is important. Benefits are made possible or produced by features and if they are relevant to someone then telling them about them is the best core content for a sales message. Benefits may be:

▌ *tangible or intangible* (in the computer example the status of being seen to have the latest and lightest machine may be as important to some people as the more tangible benefit of several hours work being done while travelling abroad);

▌ *personal* (it is valuable to me to be able to work on the move);

▌ *corporate* (it is profitable to my company for me to be able to work on the move);

▌ *important to other people someone is concerned about* (perhaps I am buying laptops for me and other members of staff and their feelings are important too).

Benefits must always be relevant. Strictly the fact that a car has a five-speed gearbox that will be more economical (feature) and cost less to run (benefit) is only an advantage if running costs actually matter. Someone buying an expensive sports car may be in a position not to care about the cost of petrol.

The task here therefore is first to look at the case you plan to make, and to analyse it in terms of its features and benefits. If you list things (benefits on the right, features on the left) then you will see how they interlock. One feature can produce several benefits (as the car's five-speed gearbox is instrumental in producing a number of things: better fuel economy, less wear and tear on the engine at high speeds and less noise too). Then you can think about how you describe them. If a benefit is spoken of in descriptive terms then it becomes that much stronger in positively affecting your case.

Benefits in action

You could say something will save you money (saving something you want to save is always a benefit, as is gaining anything positive), or that it will save money and recoup its cost in a month, or it will halve what you spend. If the description matches the circumstances of the customer and if it specifically rings bells because of how it is described then this will work best.

Consider another product example. A company sells cookery equipment to restaurants and cafes. One product is a flat grill. One feature is its size: there are various models and one has a cooking surface of 800 square centimetres. What is the benefit? It will cook a dozen eggs or six steaks simultaneously. Now most people find it difficult to conjure up 800 square centimetres in their mind's eye, but everyone who runs a restaurant will be able to imagine the eggs and steaks with no problem at all. Link the way this is described to their situation further – imagine the rush you get at breakfast time – and it makes a powerful point.

Thus if you always keep in mind what something does for or means to other people you will be able to proceed in a way that will put over a more powerful case. The phrase 'benefit-led' is used in selling and that is a good way of thinking about it. Benefits come first, features explain how that is possible and, if necessary, you can add further credibility (that is evidence or proof – something other than you saying it's good).

Top tasks
Price resistance

Everyone wants a bargain. But your product is good value for money and at the end of a meeting that has been well received you are surprised to run into a strongly voiced objection: 'It's too expensive!' You know that this comment might mean many things, from being a demand for negotiation to a comment to the effect that at that price level a decision is out of the buyer's hands, or leading up to a comparison with a competitive offering.

You do not want to appear totally inflexible or lose the business by default. How do you find out what lies behind the comment, handle the objection and move to a position from which you can close?

Here's an example. This book is called _Getting a Top Job in Sales and Business Development_ (feature). It will help you make career decisions and plan effective approaches to active career management (benefits), which will help ensure job satisfaction and adequate rewards for what you do (further benefit). Its methods are tried and tested and their presentation in training courses has received positive feedback (evidence, to which might be added a positive comment from a named delegate or training organisation). The idea of teasing out the way you put things by saying, 'Which means that...' and seeing where that takes you is a good one. Start with a feature and at the end of the line you will assuredly have a benefit, maybe more than one.

Incidentally, proof – some evidence that is objective (ie, not just you saying that it is good) – is an important component of the overall sales case you make. Never just rely on your own say so, but seek and build in evidence. This could be sheer numbers (thousands of customers can't be wrong), or tests, guarantees or standards met or complied with. We touched earlier on a car as an example. If a motor distributor tells you that a car will do 50 miles per gallon, do you believe them, or assume that some exaggeration may be involved? How about if they say independent tests in this motoring magazine show it does 50 mpg? No contest.

You can do worse than list all the things that people might obtain from your offering prior to talking to customers. Some may be classic (see the box below), others may be more individual to whatever you are selling.

What's in it for me?

As a result of agreeing with you people might be able to:

- make more money;
- save money;
- save time, effort or hassle;
- be more secure;
- sort out problems;
- be able to exploit opportunities;
- motivate others (eg, staff);
- impress people (eg, customers).

Your chosen manner

Now with the core aspects that make your case in mind, you need to think more about how to put it over. The way your message is approached is also important. For example, if, as soon as you have uttered just a few sentences it is clear that you are taking it for granted that agreement will follow, and if this seems inappropriately arrogant, then the likelihood is that it will not be taken as seriously.

The approach taken to putting over your case should be:

- _Well considered_: if it is clearly made up as you go along and without due thought or relevance to the individual customer the case will be given less credence.
- _Well projected_: it should have the courage of its convictions. Everything about the way it is expressed – language, style and argument – should add to its power.
- _Empathetic:_ in other words it should come over as respecting other people's points of view and seeing things from their perspective. This means incidentally that it should never seem 'standard', but always sound well tailored to the individual prospect.

Empathy is perhaps especially important. If it is well in evidence it prevents other elements – however persuasively put – coming over as unreasonable or 'pushy'. A balanced approach is necessary here. If everything is piled on to create more and more persuasive power, then the message becomes strident and what is being done becomes self-defeating. If persuasion is tempered with empathy then the whole becomes more acceptable.

There is a great deal more detail, of course, but if a sales message follows these principles then already it has a better chance of succeeding. Simplistically, therefore, the key factors are:

- it helps to think of persuasion as helping people to decide;
- your logic must therefore reflect theirs;
- the essence of being persuasive is to make it easy for people to make a decision, and to do so in a way that makes your suggested action seem the best choice.

A final word

In so results-driven an area as sales one further thing is clear. Those who do best tend to be those who take on board the complex nature of the sales process and who develop an understanding of it that allows them to deploy it appropriately, as was said earlier. Beyond that they also recognise that it is dynamic. No one perfects sales skills: they only excel at what is necessary today. And they must constantly fine-tune their skills to ensure they fit with market conditions and the needs – demands and expectations – of their customers.

This applies to people's success in selling as reflected in the volume and profitability of the business they bring in, and in their ability to move up the ladder and become not just excellent sales people but one of those who has a genuinely top sales job.

10 The route to the top

In sales, as for that matter in any other field, career success does not just arrive: it is actively sought and its achievement is the result of what you do. The changing world of work and the need for active career development was touched on in the Introduction and the reasons for that, which flow from the whole work environment, will not be repeated here. The message of this chapter concerns the sensible response to the need for active approaches.

There is no one thing you can do that will put your career on the fast track. There are, however, a number of approaches that you should adopt – and adopt consistently – and these together produce what can be called an active approach. The first thing is to have a clear idea of what you want to achieve.

In a world that is increasingly dynamic in almost every respect, what do you need to note about the world of work that you aim to make the stage upon which you will earn your living?

The world of work

Business pundits and economists predict a range of varying scenarios for the future of the work environment. But there is one thing that all are certain about – it will be uncertain. We live in dynamic times. The old world of job security, jobs for life, prescribed ladders of promotion and gradually increasing success and rewards has gone – replaced by talk of downsizing (and 'rightsizing' makes it sound no better), redundancy, short-term contracts, tele-working, and portfolio careers.

As you contemplate your own career, waiting for things to 'get back to normal' is simply not one of the options. The future of careers for those who do sit back is bleak, and the environment looks set to remain challenging. The American journal *Forbes* had an apt quotation in it recently: 'if you are not bloodying your nose in today's warp speed economy, we have a word for you. Dead'. No one can guarantee a successful career for themselves, and working in sales certainly offers no exception to this rule, but personal success is something that everyone can influence to some degree. Indeed it is something that you surely want to influence. We all spend a great deal of time working. It is important to make sure that those hours are as enjoyable and rewarding as possible. There is a line in one of John Lennon's songs that runs: 'Life is what happens while you are making other plans.' It encapsulates a painful thought. There is perhaps no worse situation to get into in a career – indeed in life – than one where we look back and say to ourselves: 'If only…'.

So, with no rigid, preordained career ladder to follow, careers need planning. The question is how to do it. The bad news is that there is no magic formula. Sorry, but you cannot just snap your fingers, shout 'Promotion!' and be made Sales Director overnight (or if you can please let me know how!) You can, however, make a difference if you work at it. The starting point, especially vital at the beginning of a career, is that of knowing what you want, and this needs some systematic self-analysis.

Setting a course

There are several stages of thinking that are useful:

▌ Assess your skills: you may be surprised how many you have in, for example:
   – communication;
   – influencing;
   – managing (people or projects);
   – problem solving;
   – creativity;
   – social skills;
   – numeracy;
   – special skills (everything from languages to computer usage).

▌ Assess your work values: here you should consider factors such as:
  – a strong need to achieve;
  – a need for a high salary;
  – high job satisfaction requirements;
  – a liking for doing something 'worthwhile';
  – a desire to be creative.

This could be a long list; you might add other factors, from travel to being independent or working as part of a team.

▌ Assess your personal characteristics: are you a risk taker, an innovator, or someone who can work under pressure? Consider what kind of person you are and how these character-istics affect your work situation. In sales work one factor to which this needs to relate is payment; for example with how much of a payment-by-results element would you be comfortable?
▌ Assess your non-work characteristics: such factors as family commitments, where you want to live and how much time you are happy to spend away from home.
▌ Match your analysis to the market demands: in other words consider how well your overall capabilities and characteristics fit the market opportunities; an analysis that includes how your qualifications relate to your target area. This avoids you seeking out a route that is doomed before it starts. If anything to do with computers, say, throws you, then you either have to learn or avoid areas of work dependent on a high degree of computer literacy (and, as we have seen, most areas of sales involve computers to some degree, and some demand a high level of computer skill).

With all this in mind you can set clear objectives. The old adage that if you do not know where you are going then any road will do is nowhere more true. Aim high. You can always trade down, but you may be more successful than you think and it is a pity to miss something not because it is unachievable, but only because you do not try for it.

From here on the process of managing your career progress (including your self-marketing if you will) is in the details, and the first step is to realise just that.

121

Perception is reality

Of course, progress is dependent, probably to a major degree, on performance. Whatever job you do, unless you deliver as it were, then you will have little chance of being judged able to cope with more and promotion may – rightly – allude you. Certainly this is especially true of the role of sales within marketing. But other things have an effect too.

Consider an example. A salesman is asked to manage a new initiative with a major account. It is important. There is a great deal hanging on it and it is multifaceted: something like setting up a new way of working with them that is designed to extend the sales of the full product range, say. The person may have all the necessary characteristics to do this successfully, he can do the necessary groundwork, he is thorough and forgets nothing. He balances all the various – probably conflicting – criteria and documents a sound recommendation and plan. So far, so good. Then he is asked to present it to the customer's Board or buying committee.

Now making a formal presentation is not everyone's stock in trade. Let us assume he has not done this before. He is nervous, he does not know how to prepare, put it over well, stick to the time given to him and it proves, to say the least, somewhat lacklustre. What happens? Do people say 'Never mind, it was a sound plan'? They are much more likely to take the view that the ideas themselves are suspect; perhaps they act accordingly, putting the whole thing on hold or taking some other action. And what happens next time such a project needs allocating? The person concerned may not even be in the running. The effect on his likely career is obvious enough.

This makes an important point. Many skills are rightly regarded as career skills. In other words they are not simply important in their own right: they are important to how people are seen and how they get on. Every field of work will have some such factors that are likely to be particularly important, as in fact presentation and other communication skills often are in sales.

Top tasks
Putting it in writing

All your sales experience has been in face-to-face situations. Here you are confident, a good communicator and able to put over a persuasive case and win good levels of business. A recent move has put you in a broader business development role for the first time. You have been very successful in adapting your style and approach to the more complex sales process involved, in all but one important respect. You have no experience of writing the sort of proposal documents that are necessary here. It is a task that takes you far too long, and with which you are not comfortable. Despite your powerful verbal communication skills, you find your attempts result in something too long and insufficiently clear. Gobbledegook and an over-formal style replete with officespeak are diluting the effectiveness of these proposals and sales are being lost as a result.

You have to change your style and fast. How?

Note: In a book about the sales world perhaps I may be forgiven for mentioning here my book, How to be Better at Writing Reports and Proposals – also a Kogan Page paperback – as a suitable antidote in such circumstances.

Active career management

There is a long list of skills that should be regarded in this way. In many senior jobs they include: all aspects of managing people, presentation and business writing, numeracy and, often these days, computer skills, and more general skills such as good time management. Many are to do with aspects of communication. Productivity is as important as results. Another characteristic of modern organisational life is that everyone seems to have more and more to do. Some people cope with this better than others. They are better organised. They recognise Pareto's Law – the 80/20 rule – that a comparatively small amount of activity will give rise to a large proportion of the desired outputs. Not only is their life a little less hectic or pressured, they are able to achieve more, and it shows.

Thus one area of active career management consists, as we have seen, of recognising what career skills can help you and making sure that you excel in them. One result of reading this book may be that it is much easier to form a view of the skills you should have if you do choose, or continue to pursue, a sales career.

In addition, there are a host of other factors that have an influence on how you progress. Who you know is often seen as being as important as what you know. Some people seem very well connected. But even this usually does not just happen. They probably work at it: they note their contacts, they seek out new ones, they keep in touch and recognise that this is a two-way process. And it helps.

The way ahead

We have seen that active careerists should resolve to be of no other kind, and not to rely solely on good luck. They do however take advantage of any good fortune that comes their way. And their planning and taking a positive attitude to the process makes it more likely that they can do so.

What is necessary is an all-embracing approach to what is essentially a lifelong campaign. Those who leave no stone unturned, who look at every detail of their work life in terms of the career implications of it, tend to do best. If they have thought through what they want to do and if they have clear objectives, then – while they may not achieve everything they want – they will get closer to their ideal. This is true whether you seek to make progress within one large organisation, or whether you realistically see your career changing several times as the years go by.

For the most part, careers do not happen, they are made. Sales is no hidden backwater. It deals with competition in the market place and is itself a competitive arena for those who work in it. You can do worse than start with a philosophy of active career development at the earliest phase of your career, and see your career as likely to be made primarily – by you.

What constitutes career success

Career success can be measured in various ways, certainly of course in terms of rewards. Money may not be everything, but it is important. And sales and business development can be well paid. Job satisfaction is important too. I am prejudiced, of course, but I cannot imagine a more exciting and rewarding area of business than marketing in which to work – and sales is very much a front line marketing activity. Further, as we have seen, there is a considerable range of different jobs to be done under the overall sales banner.

Mentioning this variety provides a further opportunity to comment on the concept of a 'top job'. Ultimately, 'top' can be taken as meaning just what it says. Perhaps the Sales Director – and it is inherently a director level role – inhabits the top job. But senior positions exist in spades. A National Accounts manager in a large organisation may have a bigger job than a Sales Director of a small one; certainly he or she may be responsible for bringing in higher revenue figures. If you define top job too rigorously then only CEOs would fit the bill and the number of potential top jobs is immediately seriously limited for everyone. One thing this review should make clear is that the breadth of opportunity is wide, and that there is no lack of sales posts that are important, or at senior level, however you may define them.

Sales is an area in which success can genuinely mean being 'at the top'. It can provide a combination of satisfaction and reward that is hard to match. Having said that, you still need to know how to get in, and how to get on in it.

In the current context a number of things are important, and they are discussed below.

Achieving results

Year by year success, in most jobs, is assessed through results. In sales there is no difficulty in measuring these: they are inherent in the results of the organisation, spelt out first by targets and then linking to sales revenue, profit, market share and growth. A sales person who consistently fails to achieve his or her targets will certainly not find great favour, and in many organisations this can be restated as 'will not last long'.

The first prerequisite of getting to the top is to be successful at what you do on the way. In other words, success at the job is a factor leading to success in career terms. That said, there are other factors that contribute, so always in your career you need to consider what these are. Key ones are reviewed here.

Developing skills

Sales, like marketing, may be as much art as science, but it is not all informal and creative. Real skills are involved, as we saw in the last chapter and elsewhere. You need to be aware of what you must be able to do, what you must excel at and you must look ahead, taking a view of the job you do now and where you want to go in future. Specifically:

- *Define the skills you need*: this is an ongoing process. Skills are needed as a routine now that were not even thought about 10 years ago.
- *Take action to acquire them*: whatever it takes must be done – get yourself on a course, read a book, ask a mentor, observe what others do. Methods can be formal, such as attending a course, or informal, say, making good contact with the training department and getting to sit in on their preview of a new training film. In other words, progress can be made up of both major and minor steps forward – all may be significant and it is ultimately the cumulative effect that matters.
- *Practice*: having acquired the basic knowledge about something you have to use it. Practice really does make perfect; certainly it can improve skills. In sales the frequency of contact with customers tends to provide plenty of practice. Beyond that, a case in point that makes a good example because increasingly many sales jobs, especially senior ones, demand it, is the skill of making formal presentations. You need to know the tricks of the trade. At some stage you may need to find presentations to make. Volunteer for things, use internal meetings as an opportunity to present, get yourself on committees – whatever in your work circles makes it necessary to present regularly.
- *Keep up skills*: finally do not allow any skills once acquired to atrophy. And remember that sales skill has no permanence. In other words it needs an approach that is deployed literally

customer by customer, meeting by meeting and which changes over time along with everything else in the market place. The best sales people, those most likely to get to the top, always accept this fact and take steps to make sure they never get into a rut or assume that yesterday's techniques will work on today's customers or today's on those of tomorrow.

You can usefully link this process to your recorded achievements and CV.

Acquiring experience

Everyone wants a career that progresses and which enhances his or her experience. Time alone does not automatically do this. You may be expanding experience too slowly or, at worst, simply repeating it. An active approach here is necessary too. For example, beyond your day-to-day responsibilities a variety of projects can provide additional experience. Some bosses take this view, involving their staff progressively in more and more. See what you need to know, watch for opportunities and discuss this principle with your boss.

It is almost a prerequisite of getting on to work for a manager who fosters your learning. Staying in a position where this does not happen at all, or at least shows no sign of happening, is something to consider very carefully. There must be some very strong reasons to make it worthwhile for any real period of time.

Creating the right perception of yourself

Sales, and marketing of which it is a part, are largely about perceptions. It creates an image that makes people want to buy products and services. Similarly, how someone is perceived is as important as what they do – more so in sales than in many other spheres of organisational life. In whatever sort of organisation you may work, one thing is certain: appearances count. Never mind 'don't judge a book by its cover', people do just that. How people perceive you will inevitably colour their image of you. Your image also signals something not just about what sort of person you are, but also where you sit in the office hierarchy (official and unofficial). It also signals to some people whether you are to be regarded as friend or foe, and what power you are perceived as having to promote or protect yourself. Your image affects how people treat you – whether in terms of putting people off trying to get one over on you, or encouraging their assistance for your cause.

Customers are a prime category of people in contact with those working in sales. Their perception of someone may well affect what they buy, and their feedback about the service they receive may influence others internally about the sales person who handles their account. This makes the lesson here even more important.

So, better to heed Oscar Wilde's comment: 'it is only shallow people who do not judge by appearances', and take note of the potential effect of how people see you. After all, we all have a stereotyped image of extremes such as the absent-minded boffin, the computer geek, or the office Romeo. Almost the same thing applies to images such as the grey accountant or the flamboyant advertising man, so you should certainly consider just exactly how others see you. In selling there is the danger of unwittingly fitting the stereotyped image of the 'pushy' sales people with whom no one wants to do business.

The moral is to use the fact that judgements are made (snap decisions too) and act accordingly. The result here is that you should:

▋ accept the importance of appearance;
▋ be conscious of both the positive and negative sides;
▋ actively respond to the ways people see others;
▋ strive to create and put over the right profile.

The starting point to action here involves some self-analysis. If you know how you want people to see you, then it may be easier to seek actively to achieve the effect you want. This may seem easy. You may want to look powerful, persuasive or professional. But many such fine-sounding words are in fact just umbrella terms – you must ask what does being professional, say, *really* involve? If you made a list appropriate for a sales job it might include such characteristics as being:

▋ expert;
▋ well-organised;
▋ well prepared;

▌ confident;
▌ knowledgeable;
▌ experienced;
▌ trustworthy;
▌ honest;
▌ approachable;
▌ a good listener;
▌ decisive;
▌ capable;
▌ powerful;
▌ diplomatic;
▌ a good communicator;
▌ loyal.

The above is by no means a definitive list, though many of the qualities listed are certainly important for most people. You can probably add more, including some factors that are more specific to your current job. Maybe you need to come over as financially aware, as a good negotiator or a whiz with information technology. Maybe it is important that you are professional in a more parochial sense: being seen internally to be powerful because you have the ear of someone specific on the Board, say.

In any case, several points are clear. First, however you look at it, such a list contains a number of factors: perhaps a considerable number. Secondly, for the most part the factors represent options, that is you can _choose_ to project a feeling of, say, being approachable even if this is not your natural inclination. Most people actively boost the way they are seen in some respects. You may reckon you are well organised, for instance, but still want to give an impression of even greater heights of organisation on occasion, or perhaps aim to have a particular person see you in this light (certainly dealing with customers demands such an approach).

These two factors go together. You should have clear objectives as to how you want to come over, and work at doing just that. The number of factors that you may want actively to include indicates some complexity, and you need to see the process as one of orchestrating everything together to create what you want. This may well include recognising weaknesses. If you are naturally a disaster at self-organisation, then you may need actually to get organised, and develop this as a revised part of the way you operate, rather than just seek to *appear* well organised. At the same time it is not suggested that the overall impression become too contrived, especially not obviously contrived, which would quickly become self-defeating. For the most part, all that is necessary is some slight exaggeration of characteristics to ensure they are visible where this is what you want.

Perhaps the obvious starting point with regard to personal image is literally appearance: your clothes and the other elements of personal 'show'.

Looking the part

It should be said at once that the objective here is not to stereotype you or to remove anything of real character and replace it by a universally bland image. The days of the organisation where every businessman, for example, was expected to wear the same things (plain white shirt, grey suit, black shoes and conservative tie) are largely gone, and dress now involves a much wider range of acceptable options. Women too, appearing on the corporate scene in larger numbers and more senior positions than in the past, have a wide choice. It is, however, a matter of 'horses for courses' and you need to consider what is suitable. Indeed you need to consider what 'suitable' means.

Some things are universally only sensible. I will take the example of a man (being one myself) just to allow some examples: clean shoes, a well-pressed suit and a smart tie may always be acceptable. But there are exceptions. If a jacket and slacks is what is worn in your office, so be it, then wearing that in a well-turned out way may be fine.

On the other hand there is no option but to make individual judgements. If you work in an advertising agency or some other creative company, then a suit, particularly a conventional business suit, might be regarded as wildly overdressed. Conversely there may be a good deal to be gained by being the only one in a more conservative group who dares to wear a corduroy suit or a really jazzy tie, so that may be the right action too – for some. The most important thing is to think about it. If you simply emerge bleary-eyed from bed and reach for whatever looks reasonably clean you may miss some tricks. The current trend for 'dressing down' and informal days is fine, but does make more decisions necessary. The ultimate test here for many sales people is not, in any case, how things are in their own office, but that of their customers and their attitudes.

There are things beyond clothes that need similar consideration. What you have around you also speaks volumes about you and your overall image. Certainly your office, or workstation, is a major one. It acts as a kind of billboard to those seeking to form judgements about you. This is true to an extent even in the early stages of a sales career, when you may well only have a, perhaps shared, workstation. It is even more important later when, working as, say, a sales manager, you have your own office; then signposts include:

- its location (eg, penthouse or basement);
- its size;
- its purpose (eg, accommodating just you, or with a meeting table/chairs);
- its organisation (eg, tidy or bomb site);
- its busyness (eg, whether it appears to be a place for work or relaxation);
- its contents (eg, computer and other equipment);
- its embellishments (eg, pictures on the wall).

The situation is similar with regard to yourself and your more personal accoutrements. Here again there is no one right approach or single solution to how to deal with any particular area. A balance has to be struck, and you can usefully think about how your present way of working comes over in this respect. The following list is designed to get you thinking about the implications and perhaps prompt you to think of those factors that you can yourself adjust or arrange to help create the positive image you want:

- The best computer on your desk may be good, but can you work it?
- Are six e-mail addresses making you look more important or pretentious?
- Is a fat Filofax best or a slim one?

▌ Does your electronic organiser really save you time, or will being seen to wipe out all of your telephone number list one day make you look less than efficient?

▌ Should certificates (linked to such as membership of a professional institute) be on show?

The totality of everything you gradually accumulate around you – including your choice of company car, the hotels you stay in when away on business, even which class you travel on planes and trains – all play a part in creating the image you present to others. While you can certainly become too contrived about this sort of thing, it is likely to be worse to give it too little consideration.

Each factor is worth thinking about. It is surely true, for example, that you are more likely to deliver appropriate results if you are well organised. Furthermore, you are more likely to be taken seriously if you are *seen* to be well organised. Consider some practices that give a positive impression:

▌ *Punctuality*: turning up for things on time and hitting deadlines takes some effort, but is worthwhile in terms of the impression of efficiency it creates; this is especially important with customers.

▌ *Time management*: managing your time, your projects and diary is also well worthwhile. Good time management can increase productivity significantly. So, although there is no magic formula and the secret lies in the details and creating the right disciplines, becoming good in this way is really a necessity. This makes time for taking on projects that extend your role and helps you deliver on time as well.

▌ *Tidiness:* literally *looking* well organised. Your desk, your paperwork, your briefcase (or sample and sales aids kit) all can assist you in putting over the image that you have decided upon. Preparation clearly helps.

Rather like a mediaeval army lining up on the hill overlooking the likely battlefield, you must decide the position from which you operate. Creating a position of being regarded as personally effective, well organised, confident and on top of things makes sense. Whether you want to work quietly and unobtrusively in the background, or lead from the front, how you appear is important, needs consideration and is not a matter to be left to chance.

Appearance – in all its manifestations – should not be dismissed as cosmetic irrelevance. It is an area well worth some thought. There are few rules as to how to proceed, other than that you need to work at it and take and implement a series of considered judgements to get the balance right. If people are going to see you as influential, as a power to be reckoned with in whatever way and to whatever degree you want, then the sum total of the many ways in which others perceive you must be designed to work actively for you. The objective is to directly influence how people relate to you. Simplistically, this means that if you look like a doormat, you tend to get trodden on, and if you appear to have clout, the respect you command increases.

In summary, always remember that:

▌ You only get one chance to make a good first impression (it may be a cliché, but it is true).
▌ The details matter and contribute to the total effect (for good or ill).
▌ Perception is reality: people really will judge you on appearances.
▌ Consistency of overall approach helps to build an image cumulatively so, 'it pays to advertise'.
▌ Appearance and achievement of results go together; it is no good doing well if people never look beyond a false image to see the strengths you have.

Networking

There is an old saying that it is not what you know, but who you know that leads to success. There is real truth in this. You need help: allies, mentors, advisers, those whose knowledge, help or support can smooth your route to the top.

Networking is an active process. You need to:

▌ Seek out people who can help and might be useful.
▌ Keep a record of people, inside and outside the organisation, so that you can contact them easily.
▌ Engage in activities that help you mix usefully (just one example is attending meetings of professional or trade bodies).
▌ Regard the process as a two-way street. If you are not prepared

to help others, why should they help you? It takes a little time, but it is worthwhile – to your job and your career.

Competitive and political pressures

Fact. You should recognise that, as not everyone rises equally up the ranks of an organisation, there is an adversarial element to your relations with others. Of course people can work well together in teams, but this does not negate the fact that certain people may be in competition, if not for another specific job then to be first to travel along a particular path.

Fact. The office without some office politics has not been invented. Office politics has predominantly negative connotations. The phrase itself summons up images of back-stabbing, of Machiavellian plotting and watching your back. So the only option for those working in an organisation is to recognise this and act accordingly. No one can ignore any of the realities of life and survive for long, much less prosper in what might be called 'the office jungle'.

Managers and executives are judged by results. Success, achieving the required results, may well be a constant challenge. The phrase 'the only place where success comes before work is in the dictionary' is usually attributed to Vidal Sassoon: whoever said it first it is usually true. Yet whatever work – hard work – is necessary to succeed, and whatever skills must be cultivated to back up pure application, the challenge remains, and if circumstances and people conspire to make the task more difficult, this cannot be ignored.

Now, let us be clear. There is nothing wrong with healthy competition between people. Many would claim this is good. Certainly it is human nature. Nor is friction necessarily all bad. Indeed it can act constructively. So too with office politics: it can help – or hinder – you. Whatever it does, its effects should never be regarded as 'just happening'. An active approach is necessary to minimise the negative effects that office politics may have on you, and to maximise constructive ways in which it may help you. You need to recognise that:

▌ People have a variety of personal ambitions that could put them at loggerheads with you.

▌ Some people care little how they hurt others in their striving to get on.

▌ Work is not just competitive; it is adversarial.

▌ Appearances can be deceptive (you need to identify allies and enemies).

▌ Forewarned is forearmed (you need to observe, plan and actively respond and take initiatives).

▌ You need a career plan (if you do not know where you are going any road will do, as they say).

▌ Perception is as important as fact (how you are seen is as much the basis of how you progress as what you actually do).

▌ Surmounting circumstances (and possibly opposition) takes skill – and the appropriate skills must be acquired.

So, a response to office politics must be an inherent part of active career planning. To succeed you need:

▌ to know what is going on (information really is power);

▌ the right people on your side (and to recognise and deal with the 'bad guys');

▌ good communication skills applied internally as well as with customers (this is how you relate to others within the work-place);

▌ the 'right' image or profile (and aspects of this may need creating and maintaining);

▌ the patience of a saint (and the ability to see the broad picture);

▌ sufficient assertiveness (to stand up for what you want and influence outcomes);

▌ organisational and management abilities (to achieve your work and career goals in tandem);

▌ fleetness of foot (the workplace is always dynamic – responding to change goes with the territory).

▌ a degree of ruthlessness (but one that does not dent your image).

Some would say women have to work harder than men in this area. Others remember the words of Charlotte Whitton: 'Whatever women do, they must do twice as well as men to be thought half as good.' Luckily, this is not difficult. Whatever your sex, office politics is something to be realistic about. It exists. If affects you. And the only practical response is to take an active approach to it; it is not necessary to be aggressive, it is important to be aware.

Amongst sales staff there is a built in competitiveness with regard to sales results (everyone wants to be top of the sales league). That said, and because sales people often work largely independently, there may be less competition in some other respects (unless the sales manager is about to leave and everyone reckons the job should be theirs). So, while in a geographically organised sales team you may not meet your colleagues that often, it is usually worth regarding them as of potential help. Certainly liaison around a team is a good way to freshen your sales techniques and, if what you pick up is well applied and helps your results, then improved results may enhance your image and position.

Your attitude

It should be clear from what has already been said in this chapter that you need to take a positive attitude to a range of things if you are to actively create a smooth path forward. By way of further example, consider the following three specific areas:

1. *Training.* As you cannot do most jobs or get to the top without certain skills, training is important. Most companies have a reasonable culture of training. Foster it, use it and request (insist, fight for – whatever it takes) the training you need. Being seen to welcome training, and having a planned approach to it, will be well regarded in a good organisation. So, while you may not always be able to get as much training as quickly as you would like, it should be possible to secure what you need to underpin your career plans.
2. *Appraisal.* Not every company or every manager undertakes constructive job appraisals (perhaps not least because conducting a good appraisal meeting is not easy). But however they are done in whatever organisation you may work for – make the most of them. This involves:
   - becoming familiar with the system;

- asking for an agenda and any other details you think
  relevant in advance;
- planning for the meeting (a process that goes on in a way
  all through the period before one);
- getting and noting written conclusions;
- making career planning a part of the process.

The main purpose of job appraisal is to make the next year's
(or whatever period is involved) work activity go well. But it
should look further ahead too. Appraisal meetings are, or
should be, the appraisee's meeting: have your say, make them
useful and always approach the whole thing constructively.
What comes from them may directly affect your career
progress. More detail on appraisal meeting procedure is
beyond our scope here. However, if you will forgive a plug,
my mini-book, _30 Minutes Before Your Job Appraisal_ (Kogan
Page), which is written for the person being appraised, might
be a worthwhile investment. In sales, where results are so
obvious and form therefore a naturally significant part of the
appraisal meetings content, one resolution to make is to
ensure that you direct appraisal discussion to broader issues
and this gets its fair share of the emphasis.

3. _Management._ Appraisal is in fact just one aspect of your rela-
    tionship with management. Whatever you do, you will (until
    you are Managing Director) normally report to someone. You
    will also have to work with others, for example others on the
    same level in other functions (links to production or technical
    departments are common in sales). Again your attitude to
    these relationships should be constructive and two-way. Just
    seeing what you can get from people is short-sighted. If you
    want cooperation then it is better to see it as a two-way street.

It should also be said here that, if and when you manage others,
you need to work at that management. The process of getting to
grips with being a manager takes time, effort and skill. But it is
worthwhile. As a manager you can only succeed through the
efforts of your people. Thus they become vital to your success in
your job, and therefore to your career. Look after them. A good
team is an asset to anyone's career prospects.

Success, and realism

The title of this chapter talks about a route to the top. The term implies that the route takes some time to travel along. Whatever your current position, it is as well to set yourself some goals. These can take various forms, relating for instance to:

▌ salary levels (or, in the short term, achieving other incentive payments);
▌ job grades and positions;
▌ specific types of work or involvement;
▌ ancillary factors (eg, travel).

Remember that the possible path ahead may branch, in other words a number of different routes could take you down paths that give you the experience and rewards you want. It is a good rule never to cut off your options unless you have to. Things – and feelings – change. It may be that something like the arrival of a young family changes your attitude to travel, for instance. But the alternative might be not to ignore routes that put you in a position of being away from home a lot, but to seek relocation and actually live overseas – family and all.

You have to set your sights high, but also be realistic. If you are clear what you want (and remain so despite changing circumstances) then you can chart a course forward. What you do on the way and how you enjoy that is often as important as the final goal. Having a whole list of goals that take you forward is anyway more likely to be satisfying than adopting a more simplistic approach. You may want to always look to an ultimate goal, but it is satisfying to be able to tick off some lesser ones along the way, preferably on a regular basis.

However successful you may be, and however close you get to the top (or in whatever form you reach it), the old adage that success is a journey and not a destination is worth bearing in mind. You want to enjoy the journey irrespective of where it may end, not struggle unhappily for years to achieve a brief period of satisfaction later on. At any particular point you may have a variety of views about what you have done to date and what you want to do next.

In the next chapter, we look at some of the considerations influencing how you find what is the right job for you.

11 Where to find top sales jobs

Finally, in this chapter are a few words about the process of actually finding and applying for jobs. Whether it is your first job, or your first job in sales, or you are well experienced and seeking a further step up the ladder or a move to the 'top', how you go about it is very important. Let us spell that out specifically: how you go about it can make the difference between being offered a position and falling at the first post.

This is a well-documented area. There are many books of the 'how to get a job' variety, reviewing in detail everything from the nature of CVs to the right necktie to wear at an initial interview. It is not the objective of this book to duplicate that advice, beyond a brief restatement of certain key issues.

The prerequisites of successful job seeking

Prepare a first class CV

There is no such thing as a standard CV. By that I mean that often (always?) the CV will need amending to produce the emphasis appropriate to an application for a particular job. This may seem a chore, but it is certainly worthwhile. Your CV may need to vary depending for instance on the industry in which the job exists, the size of the organisation, its location and, not least, the precise configuration of the job and the skills and experience that it is most important for an applicant to possess. It should logically, given the results-oriented nature of sales activity, concentrate on abilities and achievements. A CV should be neatly typed, and word processing makes doing this simple enough.

Compose a first class individual covering letter

While a CV can be a true reflection of someone's abilities, many are the result of advice and some are written by someone other than the applicant (eg, an agency). Employers know this, so in a small but significant way the content and tone of a letter can add to the information that is weighed in the balance to decide whether an applicant goes forward to interview stage. This is a special opportunity in this area as the experience of many managers is that sales people are not at their best when putting things in writing. If you are, then you will stand out in a positive way.

Be realistic

Employers use a variety of criteria to make the recruitment process manageable. It is said that the ideal recruitment advertisement prompts one reply – from a candidate who is both suitable and appointed. This may never happen, but the reverse, the job of analysing and screening a couple of hundred replies is a daunting, time-consuming and expensive task. The result is that invitations designed to prompt candidates to apply are intended to focus the process, securing a smaller number of applicants who are exclusively 'on spec'. It is not always the case that a non-graduate, say, to take a simple factor, could not do the job and would never be appointed. Rather it is that when an employer specifies 'graduates only' it reduces the number of applications and keeps the process manageable. So, be realistic. Apply for jobs that are stretching your credentials a little by all means – nothing ventured nothing gained. But do not hide the fact that you are somewhat off-spec (it will be seen anyway). Explain why, despite this, you feel you should be considered and ultimately do not be surprised, or resentful for that matter, if your strike rate is less with this sort of application.

Research the employer organisation

If – when! – you move to the next stage, you really must not go into an interview and ask what the company does. Employers like it if an interest has clearly been taken. It is not so complicated: get their annual report, check their Web site, send for a brochure, go – if possible – and look at their product or talk to some of their customers. The information you discover can help you decide what kind of things to raise at an interview.

Prepare for the interview

Check out good interview practice (it may well be something you have not done very often, or for a while) and prepare for each one. This means thinking through what you might be asked, what to ask, making some notes and aiming to create a link between your experience and credentials and the job itself. With something so results-oriented as sales, it is your sales results and responsibilities that will most interest people if you already have some sales experience. If not, recognise that there is no infallible test to check whether someone can sell or not, so people will look hard at anything you have done that indicates in some way that you have what it takes.

Be yourself

There is a danger that all this care and preparation may come over as a stilted approach. Employers want to know about you, the real you. Of course you want to paint a full picture and leave out nothing that might weigh in the balance in your favour, but for all the checking of details, how your competence shows through in the way you present yourself counts for a good deal too. Certainly if you appear hesitant, unsure or seem to be hiding things, that will not help.

Be honest

I remember seeing research (by a quality newspaper) that suggested that something like a quarter of applicants lie on job applications forms, and then presumably at interviews. More recently a MORI survey has explored this in depth, finding fully one-third of CVs contain deception. The details of this can be investigated on www.cvvalidation.com, a Web site specific to the survey.

Put the best face on things by all means, but resist the temptation to say you were studying for a postgraduate degree of some sort when you spent the time selling shell necklaces on a beach in Goa. It should not be surprising that many employers check, indeed this may be most likely amongst those you would consider the most desirable sort of employer.

Remember that presentation is especially important with sales and business development jobs, which are concerned, after all, with image, perceptions and how things appear. A potential employer is not just judging you as an interviewee. They will infer from your interview performance how you would come over in other contexts: at a sales meeting, a briefing meeting for major customers, or a staff meeting for what may be your sales team.

Where to find sales jobs

Beyond these brief comments, we will now turn to the question of where sales jobs can be found. Locating a job can be low key and self-contained. For example, I got my first job from the personal initiative of writing direct to a list of publishing companies. Three out of 30 replied. All said 'No'. But one of them volunteered the suggestion that I try another firm, one I had not approached. I wrote one more letter, and was offered an interview and then a job. Easy, well reasonably so, as it turned out. But success may not come so readily. As the range of sources of sales jobs is many and various, it may be prudent and useful to use more than one. This book is not a directory, so no list follows – it would quickly date. Anyway, I recently read in a management journal that there are some 5,000 job agencies urging executive job-seekers to contact them on the Internet alone and doubtless many of these claim to deal with sales positions.

What you should be clear about, however, is the differing nature of the different sources. If you are seeking a first job then such methods as university schemes and the 'Job Fairs' held by universities at which employers set up a stall to attract suitable graduates are good starting points. Later a variety of other methods are possible.

One point needs emphasising before reviewing methods. It is

impossible to know where your next job will come from. To a large extent job hunting is a numbers game. The more bread you put on the waters as it were, the more likely it is that something suitable will materialise sooner rather than later. Of course, you may be lucky. Sometimes it happens like that: you see a suitable advertisement, apply and get the job with no more needing to be done. But it is best to assume this will not happen. Consider how fast you need to move. Circumstances differ. You may be content to keep a few things on the boil for some months and see what happens. You may need to spread the net wide to encourage success in the short term.

Avoid one mistake that can cost you a lot of time: hanging on for something that looks just right but is slow to come to fruition. It can take time while an application is progressed. You write, you attend an interview, you are put on a short list, you attend another interview, references are checked, you wait — the process can run on for weeks, if not months. It is easy to allow enthusiasm, and perhaps confidence too, to lull you into a false sense of security. You become sure it is 'in the bag'. If the final outcome is not successful and you have not continued other activity so that you have other prospects at, say, interview stage, then you lengthen the whole process. The moral is simple: keeping a number of balls in the air at one time is likely to get you the job you want soonest, and if you end up being offered two, then you can take the best.

Back to methods and sources of sales and marketing jobs. Let us start with the least formal.

Networking

It is said that it is not what you know, but who you know that counts. It can be true of job seeking, and some people get jobs through the intelligence they pick up from others (and occasionally direct from such a contact). Networking implies a systematic approach to creating and maintaining contact with people; in this case people who might be potential sources of jobs or job-related information. Consider who you know (friends, family, work colleagues past and present, customers and competitors, professional contacts – and that guy you met at the conference you attended in London). Keep in touch and consider

mechanisms for keeping in touch. Some people you might tell
outright – 'I'm after a new job.' Some you might write to, telephone or e-mail. Consider also group situations: where might you
meet useful people? One example is at national or local meetings
of professional or industry bodies (see 'Useful addresses and
information', the next chapter). While looking for a job, you may
want to attend such things a little more regularly for a while, get
onto a committee or encourage an invitation for you to be a
meeting speaker.

Make notes, keep records, plan activity and follow up.
Remember that networking consists not just of you seeking
benefit from others: it is a two-way street. Viewing it constructively as such will ultimately let you get more from it.

Events

A variety of events cater for the job seeker, especially at start-out
level. These range from the events staged by potential employers
in colleges and universities to commercial events held like any
other exhibition and typically held in exhibition venues.

On-spec applications

This is often rejected as having a low strike rate. So be it. But if you
have set your sights on something very specific it does make sense
and, provided the approach is professional, can bring success.
Timing is clearly a factor here: given the time, effort and cost of
recruitment, if your approach arrives when a vacancy does exist it
makes sense for the employer to check you out.

Media advertising

The sensible job seeker in any field scours the media. Marketing is a
major function of business and sales is both an important part of it
and a people-intensive one; it is thus a category of job that features
in many media. It is worth reviewing the media systematically:

▌ *National press*: the main newspapers to watch are the *The Daily
Telegraph* (which has a major share of the sales vacancy market),
The Times and *The Guardian*; also the quality Sundays.

▌ *Regional and local papers:* these are used extensively by those looking to recruit people living in the area of a territory they are looking to staff, and by smaller companies.

▌ *Magazines:* one category is especially worth noting – the trade press of particular industries. The more specialised an industry is (or where people in it regard it as such) the more likely it is that their specialist press will be used for appointments advertisements. In publishing, for example, *Publishing News* or *The Bookseller* are probably as likely to be used as national papers.

▌ *Internet advertising:* here I make a difference between sites on the Internet that display job advertisements, leaving it to the individual to apply direct to the employer, and those (see below) that have an interactive element or describe themselves as agencies.

▌ *Internet agencies:* like so much else to do with the Internet and e-commerce they change as you watch and no attempt is made here to list even a selection. For all the activity in this sector, the more worthwhile appointments still seem to be more traditionally advertised. By all means search the Web, but you will need to do so selectively or time will allow nothing else. Sites with a narrow focus are perhaps the best priority.

▌ *Recruitment agencies:* these are many and various and certainly too numerous to list here (details of the definitive reference, a directory called *Executive Grapevine*, appear in the next chapter). Some points are worth making, however. Recruitment agencies come in all shapes and sizes. A large general agency may have specialist sections, and deal with marketing – and sales – as a discreet sector. Others may specialise: by level of appointment, by industry or sector, geographically, whatever. Either may be right for you. Larger agencies offer a broad spread of positions, specialists may focus on the specific area you want. Some recruiters are better informed than others, of course, but it makes sense to start from the basis that you will be in contact with someone who does understand the industry and other details specific to a particular appointment.

There is a danger in viewing agencies as 'all the same'. They are not, and nor are the consultants who staff them. You will fare best with them if you remember this, do your homework and tailor your approaches and contacts with them as much as possible.

▌ *Headhunters*: or to describe them more properly, executive search agencies. It should be said at once that these only operate in the sales area at the most senior level. Then they operate on the basis of taking a brief from employers and 'searching' in an individual way, normally with no formal advertising of any sort, for suitable candidates. They then interview and take the process through as required, much as many other agencies do. They operate exclusively at senior (or specialised) levels, and their mode of operation is therefore geared to represent employers rather than job seekers. Nevertheless it is possible to register with some of them; though how much use this proves to be is dependent, of course, upon the assignments they are commissioned to undertake.

If adopting a 'leaving no stone unturned' approach suits, and you are in or ready for the senior echelons, then headhunters may be a group worth pursuing. Like so much else these days, contact is often possible through Web sites. There are too many search firms to list here, but you might check Spencer Stuart & Associates, one of the large international firms, on www.spencerstuart.com. The site has a specific facility to lodge your CV with them, and provides an example of how these things work. This is one to file away for the future perhaps as you aim to make the jump to the topmost rung of the ladder.

▌ *Specialist services*: ways of providing assistance to both job seekers and employers change progressively, as those originating and marketing such services take action to create advantage in the market place. Internet agencies are comparatively new; further new methodologies will no doubt appear. You need to keep an eye on what is happening here and be ready to use the right services when your situation demands this sort of assistance. On the one hand active job seeking demands that you spread the net wide to increase the chances of success. On the other hand you have to be realistic and keep things manageable. Compromise again – but do not get yourself into a position where you despair of ever finding the right thing and are just not taking sufficient action to make success likely.

The key here has a strong parallel with marketing a product or service. You must see what needs to be done as 'self-marketing', as selling yourself. You must decide on a suitable mix of methodology and go about everything that entails in a professional way. You may also need to be persistent and take the long view: your ultimate aim is worth taking both time and effort to achieve.

Whatever you do to get the job you want, and thereafter to get on in it, it is worthwhile. Many people would describe sales and business development as a particularly interesting, potentially exciting, and worthwhile career. Certainly any success you have is going to be a direct reflection of your own efforts: that is the nature of the process.

Selling, in all its forms, has a role that is at the sharp end of volatile market places. In whatever context sales skills are deployed, it is a role that acts to make things happen. And it never stands still – creatively and innovatively helping to make it continue to act effectively in increasingly dynamic market places may be just the challenge you want. Go for it, and do so using your sales and marketing skills. And when you do – aim high. I wish you well.

Useful addresses and information

Whatever stage of your career you are at you may need information or advice. The following is designed to highlight key sources of information about sales and business development (and to link beyond that to some extent to marketing). The entries fall into three categories:

1. *Professional and advisory bodies:* these encompass those that offer qualifications, training, some sort of appointments service, and are simply sources of information and networking (this latter sometimes on a local basis through their regional branches).
2. *Magazines and journals:* containing news of marketing matters, reports and advice on marketing methods and techniques and, in some cases, job advertisements.
3. *Recruitment agencies* (or rather how to access them).

1. Professional and advisory bodies

We will start with the 'umbrella' body for the area of which sales and business development are constituent parts.

Chartered Institute of Marketing
Moor Hall
Cookham
Maidenhead
Berks SL6 9QH
Tel: 01628 427190
www.cim.co.uk

This is listed first as a prime source of reference. As an overall summary the Institute describes itself thus:

The Chartered Institute of Marketing (CIM) is the professional body for marketing, with over 60,000 members worldwide.

Founded in 1911, it has been instrumental in elevating marketing to a recognised, respected and chartered profession.

It is the only marketing body able to award Individual Chartered Marketer status to eligible members. Chartered Marketer status is a professional standard that reflects an individual's commitment to developing their professional skills in an increasingly competitive marketplace.

As an examining body for over 60 years, the Institute's Certificates and Postgraduate Diploma (DipM) are internationally recognised qualifications, available through a worldwide network of educational institutions and distance learning providers.

It is worth mentioning the Institute's services:

▋ *Career development services.* These include a range of information in booklet form or downloadable from their Web site, a Career Advice Line (Tel: 01628 427322), a Career Counselling service (run in collaboration with Connaught Executive via a network of 25 offices around the country (Tel: 01628 427322 initially) and two routes for those seeking new jobs. The first is JobFocus accessed through the Institute's Web site and available to all, the second (for members only) is the Job Vacancy Database run with Quantum Consulting Group and accessed via www.cim.co.uk/membership-net.
▋ *The library and information service.*
▋ *The qualifications they themselves offer.*
▋ *The network of branches.* These mean no one is far from a local source of information and networking. There are a number of overseas branches also and the Institute links with the European Marketing Confederation with associate bodies in 24 countries within and outside the European Union (total membership is more than 300,000); its Web site is www.emc.be.
▋ *CIM Direct.* A source of business books for purchase.

In addition the Institute is the parent body for the Institute of Professional Sales (see below), which undertakes a parallel role to its parent, focusing solely on the sales function, and CAM Foundation (Communication, Advertising and Marketing) which is the umbrella body for qualifications across the various marketing disciplines; www.camfoundation.com.

CIM has two Web sites: www.cim.co.uk, its main site, has been recently upgraded and another, www.ConnectedinMarketing.com has been added to specifically assist those involved in e-business.

Note: while this is a source of value to all, you should be aware that some of the services listed above are available only to members of the Institute.

The Institute of Professional Sales
This describes itself as follows:

> The vision of IPS is to create an Institute that recognises both the achievement of professional qualifications and the value of experience.
>
> Its aim is to bring together the knowledge of academia, the skills of training organisations, the experience of practitioners with the motivation essential for all selling roles.
> The objective of IPS is to raise the profile of sales people and to gain recognition for the sales function. In addition, we want to create a very clear training path for those coming in to sales.
>
> Additionally, we wanted to provide events and networking opportunities and to define and evolve 'best practice' in sales.
>
> Successful selling is essential for any business and the Institute of Professional Sales aims to make selling an accurately defined science rather than just an acquired art. All the qualifications are based on the National Standards together with the real life experience of first class trainers.
>
> The corporate benefits offered are that IPS will recognise training by external companies and help to raise the profile of the sales profession within those companies. IPS is dedicated to raising standards of best practice, is compatible with Investors in People and encompasses many industry leaders.

150

Individual benefits of joining IPS include use of the designatory letters, advice on career development, *Winning Business* magazine, an active Regional Events programme and access to the Information and Library Service.

For more information on IPS, visit the Web site: www.iops.co.uk or e-mail the Institute:michaelwarne@iops.co.uk. It can be contacted at the same address as The Chartered Institute of Marketing (see above).

Other useful bodies include:

The Marketing Society
St George's House
3/5 Pepys Road
London SW20 8NJ
Tel: 020 8879 3464
www.marketing-society.org.uk

It describes itself as 'the premier organisation in the UK for senior marketing professionals and general managers of marketing oriented companies'. It states its purpose as to provide access to the best network for the leading edge ideas and practice and to inspire and support Society members by encouraging debate and contact between them. It is a long established and well-respected body, with something of a bias towards FMCG companies; it has a quarterly journal, *Market Leader.*

The PM Forum
Warnford Court
29 Throgmorton Street
London EC2N 2AT
Tel: 020 7786 9786
www.pmint.co.uk

This networking group is linked to the journal *Professional Marketing* and has a focus on the marketing of professional services (and a sister group concerned with financial services marketing).

151

The Professional Services Marketing Group
PO Box 353
Uxbridge
UB10 0UN
Tel: 01895 256972

This is similar to The Marketing Society, but is exclusively for those working in the professional services sector (with firms such as accountants, lawyers, surveyors, architects, consultants, etc). Its main activity is through member meetings of various sorts. There is a Web site: www.psmg.co.uk.

2. Magazines and journals

There are many magazines covering the marketing area, either from a general perspective or with a focus on one specific subsection of marketing, but only a few are of significance and focus on sales.

Winning Business
Quest Media Ltd
9 The Leathermarket
Western Street
London SE1 3ER
Tel: 020 7378 1188

This is probably the most useful magazine in the field, and not only because I write for it regularly. The publishers describe it thus:

> *Winning Business* is a leading edge, bi-monthly magazine published in association with the Institute of Professional Sales, targeted at and read by senior managers within organisations that have responsibility for customer facing aspects of their business, such as sales, marketing and customer service. The uniqueness of the publication relates to the fact that it is the only 'how to' focused magazine in the UK that provides senior management with advice, guidance and inspiration to help them win more business.

The editorial of the magazine is designed to be of interest to any business leader interested in finding, winning, retaining and growing business.

The benefits of publishing a magazine that has many of Europe's top business experts writing for it, has enabled the editorial team to build a framework of key business principles around which content is developed. This approach means looking at the subject of how organisations find, win, retain and grow business from three very specific areas, people, processes and technology.

The magazine aims to explore how organisations develop and evolve their people and their processes to increasingly meet and exceed the needs and expectations of customers whilst using technology to enable the changes and developments they wish to make. The other key principle is to encourage organisations to increasingly integrate the different functions of the organisations, particularly their sales, service and marketing operations in order to improve the consistency and the quality of the experience for the customer.

This consistent framework enables the magazine to build on and broaden the range of issues and subjects it addresses whilst continuously questioning the validity of any new ideas and concepts against its core principles.

To achieve its objectives _Winning Business_ brings together global experts on sales, service and marketing. They write to a tight brief, resulting in easily accessible, knowledgeable and authoritative editorial that consistently shows its readers how to succeed in their efforts to find, win, retain and grow business with their profitable customers.

The magazine is packed full of advice, ideas, best practice and research identifying and exploring the best and most effective ways for organisations constantly to improve their performance. By providing a reader-friendly package of high quality, interesting, practical, and thought-provoking advice in an expertly written, well-designed format, the magazine captures the attention of senior business leaders, influencing the opinion formers.

Sales Director
www.saleszone.co.uk

This is also useful and has very much the style and format of something like the journal *Management Today*.

Sales & Marketing Management
www.salesandmarketing.com

The main US magazine on the subject, broader than solely sales management and containing useful material.

Sales & Marketing Professional
This is the journal linked to the Institute of Sales & Marketing Management. Somehow this has always remained in the shadow of the main institutes; its base is sales, but it seems to think marketing is more sexy and positions itself 'higher'.

All the above are specific, but it is worth bearing in mind that, as selling is an essential part of the marketing mix, marketing journals feature articles on selling and sales management from time to time. The Library at the Chartered Institute of Marketing will produce lists of recent articles on request, though there is a charge to non-members.

Finally, for a general overview of marketing issues (which inevitably touches on sales and business development as a topic), the CIM journal is worth noting.

Marketing Business
Exmouth House
3–11 Pine Street
London EC1R 0JH
Tel: 020 7923 5400

3. Recruitment agencies

This is, as has been mentioned, too large a category to list; however there is one key reference that is worth mentioning and which is the definitive guide:

Executive Grapevine
2nd Floor, New Barnes Mill
Cottonmill Lane
St Albans
Herts AL1 2HA
Tel: 01727 844335
www.executive-grapevine.co.uk

This lists agencies of all sorts and information can be accessed in various ways: by industry and work area; the exact nature of each firm is made clear. First published at the end of 2000, this directory is subtitled: _The business of international marketing._

There is, of course, a wealth of other, more general, sources of information without a specific sales and marketing focus. Appointments advertisements appear in many newspapers, but in the UK _The Daily Telegraph_ probably gets the majority of choice sales appointments. It is also worth looking at the regional press as territory-based jobs and those with companies based locally are certainly advertised in these. Beyond that there is a range of journals; for example, _The Economist_ carries senior appointments, some of which will be in business development aspects of marketing. Other magazines, for example _Management Today,_ may give space to marketing issues, amongst other matters.

Glossary

At this stage, if you are currently outside the business or new to it, you will be aware that sales and business development encompass a wide range of activity. Describing this multifaceted activity and the techniques involved in its execution has created a good deal of jargon. If you seek to pursue the idea of such a career, or extend the one you are currently embarked upon, then you may well need – as has been made clear through these pages – to study further in a variety of ways to keep abreast of all that is involved. For those at an early stage the following short glossary will, while not attempting to be comprehensive, clarify some of the main jargon terms. (If you want to put this in the context of marketing as a whole, then you might note that my book *Everything You Need to Know About Marketing*, which presents a brief and light-hearted overview of the marketing process, ends with a glossary of marketing terms. This is also a Kogan Page paperback.)

account Essentially a customer, most usually used of a customer which is an organisation and which has more than a one-off order relationship with the supplier.

benefits The focus of sales messages, benefits are the things a product or service will do for or mean to a customer (rather than the features, which are the factual things about it). For example, a car may have a five-speed gearbox, rather than a four-speed one (a feature), producing benefits including good fuel economy and less wear and tear on the engine at high speeds.

call frequency The number of times a regular customer is called on (eg, once a month).

call planning The preparatory thinking, indeed any preparation, that should proceed making a customer call.

call reports A report on an individual sales call, noting activity and results.

closing The term applied to the final stage of the sales interview or process, which ties things down and aims to obtain a commitment.

cold calling Making an initial approach to a prospect where there has been no prior contact (this may be done in person or on the telephone).

commission The element of a remuneration package paid in a direct link with sales results; most usually paid in money (*see* incentives).

customer Someone who has purchased a product. Some businesses, especially services, talk of clients, and in less guarded moments there are those who will refer to punters (or worse).

detailing Certain industries use individual terminology to describe the sales interview in their field. For example pharmaceutical companies do not sell to doctors: they detail them.

export selling This describes the sales job done in international marketing that demands regular visits to an overseas market (or markets); the term usually describes only people resident in their home market and travelling to others.

features *See* benefits.

incentives Payments, often in non-financial form (eg, holidays), linked to aspects of sales results. They can be very focused, for example a quarterly scheme might link to the number of new accounts opened or sales of a particular product.

kerbside conference A meeting held to analyse the way a sales call has gone, often between a sales manager and an individual member of the sales team (so called because it often takes place in the car).

major customers This term usually refers to large customers, that is large compared with others of the same company rather than of any particular inherent size (a variety of names are used here, including Key Accounts).

major sales A sale where the size of the individual order is large (again compared with the average for a particular customer). Often the lead-time of obtaining such sales is long.

needs Customer needs and their identification – finding out what customers want and why – is an inherent part of the sales process.

negotiation The skill that fits alongside selling. Simply selling gets people to make an agreement, and negotiation arranges the terms and conditions (and price factors) on which matters will proceed. It is a key skill for many people in sales.

objections Reasons voiced by prospective customers as to why they should not buy. They may or not take the form of questions – handling objections is an essential sales technique.

pitch (or sales pitch) Pitching describes the process of going after business from a particular prospect; it usually refers to complex sales processes, especially those necessitating a formal presentation or written proposals.

proposal Normally a written document that sets out the precise recommendation in areas of non-standard products and services (something I have to write regularly in selling training). It will also specify costs. A quotation is a document that sets out little information beyond the costs.

prospect Someone who is a potential customer, but who has not bought yet.

prospecting The task of identifying and making contact with potential new customers.

qualifying leads (or prospects) The process of analysis that sorts the sheep from the goats in terms of deciding which of a large number of prospects are priorities and provide the greatest chance of a sale being made.

quotation *See* proposal.

representative Another word for sales person (now rather old fashioned).

sales aids Anything from graphs and pictures to brochures, computers, or the product itself that is used to assist the sales process and shown to customers during a sales meeting.

sales management The management function that manages and directs the team of people working in sales; can be at Board level – hence Sales Director. Often there is a regional structure of Area Managers to cover the whole country.

sales productivity The organisational process that makes sales activity productive and includes such factors as planning sales time and analysing the ratios that constitute success.

sales records The records of customers used primarily to guide future action and manage continuity by those who regularly contact large numbers of customers.

sales targets The figures (of everything from the number of customers to be contacted to the amount to be sold in a period) to which sales people must work; sometimes referred to as quotas.

selling Personal, one-to-one, persuasive communication whether done by sales people or others and whether done face-to-face or, say, on the telephone.

telephone selling The overall term for all contact on the telephone, it encompasses many different things including the sales side of someone handling service aspects of customer contact in a sales office or call centre, through to full-time cold calling activity.

telescript Literally a script to be followed by those selling on the telephone; this reduces flexibility and is not to be recommended as a general rule.

territory The geographic area managed by an individual responsible for sales to customers 'on their patch'.

USP Or 'unique selling proposition'; it is the key, core description (in benefit terms) that gives a particular product its appeal. It might be said that if there is no USP, there is likely to be no sale.

Note: the above terms are exclusive or special to selling, but as the sales process is essentially a communication skill, so other terms reflecting this are much used.

Index

NB: page numbers in *italic* indicate figures.